# CONTENTS

# PART FOUR

## CRITICAL HISTORY

# PART FIVE

## BACKGROUND

# PART ONE

## INTRODUCTION

## HOW TO STUDY A POEM

Studying on your own requires self-discipline and a carefully thought-out work plan in order to be effective.

- Poetry is the most challenging kind of literary writing. In your first reading you may well not understand what the poem is about. Don't jump too swiftly to any conclusions about the poem's meaning.

- Read the poem many times, and including out loud. After the second or third reading, write down any features you find interesting or unusual.

- What is the poem's tone of voice? What is the poem's mood?

- Does the poem have an argument? Is it descriptive?

- Is the poet writing in his or her own voice? Might he or she be using a persona or mask?

- Is there anything special about the kind of language the poet has chosen? Which words stand out? Why?

- What elements are repeated? Consider alliteration, assonance, rhyme, rhythm, **metaphor** and ideas.

- What might the poem's **images** suggest or symbolise?

- What might be significant about the way the poem is arranged in lines? Is there a regular pattern of lines? Does the grammar coincide with the ending of the lines or does it 'run over'? What is the effect of this?

- Do not consider the poem in isolation. Can you compare and contrast the poem with any other work by the same poet or with any other poem that deals with the same theme?

- What do you think the poem is about?

- Every argument you make about the poem must be backed up with details and quotations that explore its language and organisation.

- Always express your ideas in your own words.

These York Notes offer an introduction to the poetry of John Keats and cannot substitute for close reading of the text and the study of secondary sources.

> **CONTEXT**
>
> The word 'poetry' comes from the Greek word *poesis*, meaning 'making' or 'creating'. People have been writing poetry for thousands of years – the earliest we have dates back to c. 3000BC.

# READING KEATS'S POETRY AND LETTERS

'I think I shall be among the English Poets after my death,' John Keats boldly declared to his brother George in a letter of October 1818. He had not yet turned twenty-three. His confidence is startling when we consider that he had just been telling George about some extremely hostile reviews of his work. Such hostility, Keats assured him, was 'a mere matter of the moment' (*Letters* 1, p. 394). He was right.

In his brief creative career, brought to an end at twenty-five by his death from tuberculosis, Keats produced some of the greatest and most enduring poems in the English language. While literary fashions have changed many times since his death, and literary **canons** repeatedly made and unmade, Keats's position 'among the English poets' has remained secure. What, then, are the qualities in his work that have made it so impervious to the vagaries of literary taste? It is difficult to attribute Keats's continuing popularity to any one particular characteristic. The Keats we read with such pleasure today is not the same Keats who was appreciated in the past: 'Keats' has meant many different things to different people.

During the Victorian age he was read for his luxuriant and sensuous language, for the striking pictorial effects of such poems as 'The Eve of St Agnes'. By the end of the nineteenth century, Keats was acclaimed as the forerunner of the **art for art's sake** movement. Following this, when the widespread reaction of the 1920s and 1930s against nineteenth-century poetry tarnished the reputations of the other **Romantic** poets, Keats sailed through with his position 'among the English poets' secure. He was seen as the poet of 'aesthetic experience', and the focus was on the forms and structures of his poetry, his language and his imagery. He was considered less absorbed than other Romantics with the political events of his time, and more concerned with 'universals'. Keats consequently seemed to offer the ideal material for **formalist** critics who believed that a good poem was organically coherent and self-contained, that poetry should be studied for its unity of form and content, and without reference to any external considerations, social, political, or biographical. Such a view of Keats has been generally rejected in the second part of the twentieth century. The formalists have been accused of accepting uncritically and reproducing methodologically

> **CONTEXT**
>
> The Romantic period is generally considered to begin around 1789, with the Storming of the Bastille and the start of the French Revolution, and to end in 1837 when Victoria ascends the throne.

one of the ideals of Romanticism. New historicist critics argue that, as the Romantic poets searched for some essential, eternal truth and beauty which transcended the mortal world of change and process, so the formalist critics suggest through their readings that poetry can, by its very nature, offer some 'universal' truths which transcend the conflicts and divisions of its historical moment.

The nature of poetry and the poet is probably the central issue in Keats's work and the opposition between the eternal **transcendent** moment and the transient human condition one of the main oppositions around which his poems are structured. It is, therefore, useful to have these different views of poetry in mind when reading Keats. Does Keats believe that poetry, the imaginative processes, can reach some universal truths? Alternatively, does he ultimately recognise that poetry is inevitably, even if not overtly, marked by the defining characteristics of its time and place and that the imagination, in suggesting the accessibility of something more enduring and essential, is deceptive? Keats quite frequently follows the pattern of presenting a speaker who moves into an imaginative oneness with some object of contemplation which he sees as embodying that transcendent world. Ultimately, however, the speaker finds it necessary to return to, as he says in 'Ode to a Nightingale', the 'sole self' (line 72), to the transient world full of sorrow and despair. In poems which demonstrate such a pattern, including 'Ode to a Nightingale' and 'Ode on a Grecian Urn', how does Keats position himself with regard to the transcendent world he leaves behind? Is he regretful? Is he sceptical of what he believed he attained?

The majority of critics today would consider Keats's attitude to be marked primarily by scepticism and, perhaps, by a touch of nostalgia for what has been desired but found illusory. The new 'Keats' who has emerged over the last twenty years is a politicised, historicised poet, a poet whose work is marked not by unity, harmony, synthesis, but by polarities, irreconcilable oppositions, and, above all, doubt. Rather than resolving oppositions and creating unity out of **paradox**, he is now seen as being torn apart by the very impossibility of reconciling contradictory impulses and desires. There has been a general interest in recovering the more sceptical and ironic voice of Romanticism, a voice marked by a distrust of the imagination and of transcendental claims concerning essential truths. In this respect, most of the later twentieth-century

 **CHECK THE NET**

For online research tools, reviews, excerpts from publications about the Romantic period, look at Romantic Circles: **http://www.rc.umd. edu/.**

critics who write on Keats see him as the most modern of all the Romantic poets. He is considered sceptical of transcendent yearnings, of romantic escapism, and insistent on the need to accept the natural world, the human condition. As he wrote to his friend John Hamilton Reynolds in July 1819: 'I have of late been moulting: not for fresh feathers & wings: they are gone, and in their stead I hope to have a pair of patient sublunary legs' (*Letters* 2, p. 128). It is this 'moulted' Keats who is in ascendance today, the poet with 'sublunary legs' rather than 'feathers and wings'.

There are two main lines of thought concerning this new down-to-earth and sceptical Keats. Some critics find a clear evolution in his poetic thought, and trace a line of development that can be loosely characterised by three main stages:

Stage 1 involves an aesthetic idealism marked by an overwhelming awareness of the impermanence and despair of the human condition and a desire to reach some essential unchanging truth through the visionary imagination. Beauty is seen as the sensuous, temporal embodiment of such transcendent truth, some unknown reality beyond the world of experience. This stage is identified with such early work as *Endymion. A Poetic Romance*.

In Stage 2 there is a growing scepticism about the powers of the imagination. In the great odes of 1819, and in such poems as 'The Eve of St Agnes', Keats considers his early aesthetic ideals with scepticism, but perhaps also nostalgia.

 **CHECK THE NET**

For a sampler of the cd on Romanticism, edited by David S. Miall and Duncan Wu, look at: **http://www.ualberta.ca/dmiall/romacdinf.htm.**

In Stage 3 he is finally reconciled with the human condition, with process and change. Keats has moved completely beyond the yearning for essential beauty and truth. Now agony is caused by ignorance, rather than by the transience and sorrow of the human condition. What the poet seeks above all is knowledge. This stage is most directly associated with 'The Fall of Hyperion', where the true poet is one whose knowledge of human suffering allows him to function as physician to the world.

In opposition to those who see this clear and straightforward progression of thought, other critics have argued that Keats's poetic career reveals a constant **dialectic**. They identify a series of vacillations between such polarities as:

- a longing for the escapist world of romance and a sceptical view of romance

- a belief in the imagination and an awareness of the deceptiveness of the imagination

- an openness to all sensations and a longing for fixed knowledge

- the desire for amoral detachment and the desire for a clear moral position

- the yearning for some essential unchanging truth and beauty and acceptance of the impermanence of the human condition

After studying the poems and reading the more detailed discussions of such themes in the section on **Critical approaches**, you should be able to determine your own position in the debate and consider how arguments could be made for both sides of the question.

While the new historicised and sceptical Keats is very different from the aesthetic poet constructed by previous generations, this does not mean we should ignore his aesthetic qualities and concentrate only on his ideas. Perhaps the best way to read and appreciate Keats's poetry is to follow what would appear to be his own dominant strategy in the writing of it. As he declared to his publisher John Taylor in 1818: 'I have been hovering for some time between an exquisite sense of the luxurious and a love for Philosophy' (*Letters* 1, p. 271). In reading Keats, maybe we too should hover.

Of all the Romantic poets Keats is in some ways the most amenable to being read for his 'philosophy'. His thought is speculative, marked by creative tensions. He never seems to preach to us or insist upon our acceptance of any particular insight. This offers quite a contrast to, say, Wordsworth whose poetic persona is authoritative, even, Keats thought, bullying and whose moments of doubt only intensify the ultimate affirmation of his beliefs. The Keatsian 'I', rather than resolving doubts and moving towards a clear didactic position, asks us to consider possibilities rather than insisting on our acceptance of any particular insight.

Keats is also the most rewarding of the Romantic poets to read for his 'luxurious' language and **imagery**. Although he constantly deals

 **CHECK THE NET**

For an index of Romantic related sites, look at **http://www. english.upenn.edu/ ~mgamer/Romantic/ index.html.**

with such abstract ideas and issues as Beauty and Truth, his poetry itself is rarely abstract and he rarely generalises. Instead, he conveys his ideas through powerfully dramatic scenes, highly concrete and specific images and vivid sense impressions. The rich sensuousness of his language, his masterful use of the image, his ability to convey the most abstract of ideas in the most concrete and vividly pictorial forms: these are his qualities which remain the most immediate, while not the only, attractions.

**CHECK THE NET**

An article on the relationship between Keats and Fanny Brawne is available from the English History Net: **http://englishhistory. net/keats/ fannybrawne.html.**

This introduction began with a confident Keats assured of his place within literary tradition. It should be added, however, that such confidence was by no means typical of him. More frequently, his letters and poems suggest anxiety and insecurity about the way his poetry would be received after his death. There are, for example, the bleak thoughts he confided to Fanny Brawne (in a letter of 1820), at a time when he was already aware he would not live much longer: 'If I should die … I have left no immortal work behind me – nothing to make my friends proud of my memory – but I have lov'd the principle of beauty in all things, and if I had had time I would have made myself remember'd' (*Letters* 2, p. 263). Anxiety and insecurity about his achievements are perhaps even more poignantly conveyed in his final direction to his friend Joseph Severn that his tombstone should carry the words: 'Here lies one whose name was writ in Water'. This time, Keats was wrong.

# PART TWO

# THE POEMS

## NOTE ON THE TEXT

*The text used in compiling these Notes is the Heinemann Poetry Bookshelf edition of* Keats: Selected Poems and Letters *(1996), selected by Robert Gittings and edited by Sandra Anstey, though this often gives only extracts of the longer poems, which are treated in full in these Notes. The edition of the letters referred to throughout is Hyder Edward Rollins's* Letters of John Keats, 1814–1821, *2 volumes, Harvard University Press, 1958. Three volumes of Keats's poetry were published during his lifetime:* Poems *(1817),* Endymion *(1818), and* Lamia, Isabella, The Eve of St Agnes and Other Poems *(1820). Many other poems remained unpublished until after his death. Poem titles in the following summaries are followed by the date of composition and, in parentheses, the date of first publication; this will either alert you to the volume in which it first appeared or indicate posthumous publication.*

## ENDYMION. A POETIC ROMANCE 1817 (1818)

- This poem of four books is based on the Greek legend of Endymion, the shepherd who gained immortality through his love for Cynthia, the moon goddess.
- To attain his ideal, Endymion must be initiated into the mysteries of the earth, the seas and the heavens.
- He returns to earth and meets an Indian Maid with whom he falls in love.
- Choosing human love over the ideal, he passes the last test in his initiation and attains his dream.

Book 1 begins with one of Keats's best-known lines, 'A thing of beauty is a joy forever': it is this eternal beauty that is the object of Endymion's quest. On Mount Latmos, a priest conducts the rites of worship associated with the rural fertility god, Pan. The worshippers call upon the god to allow them to transcend mere

**CHECK THE BOOK**

In a letter of 10 September 1817, Keats describes to his sweetheart Fanny Brawne how in Greek legend, the moon descended from the sky to admire a 'handsome young shepherd' who little thought that 'such a beautiful Creature as the Moon was growing mad in Love with him – However so it was'. See Rollins, *Letters of John Keats.*

earthly existence. Following this ceremony, the shepherd prince Endymion confesses to his sister Peona that he has fallen in love with a mysterious maiden who has come to him three times in his dreams: from the sky, from a well and in a cave. This maiden, unknown to him, is Cynthia, goddess of the moon. Now he must search for her in these places: in the regions of air, water and earth. He prepares to depart on his quest for his visionary love.

Book 2 sees Endymion descending into the depths of the earth. A golden butterfly leads him to a fountain at the mouth of a cavern and then vanishes. A naiad then appears, declaring that Endymion must travel further and suffer more before he can meet his love. He calls upon the goddess to help him, and a voice orders him to descend into the cavern. He comes across Adonis among his cupids and Venus herself appears and promises he will achieve happiness if he continues to obey. He prays for deliverance to Jove, whose eagle carries him to a secluded spot where he meets the lady of his dreams. She soon leaves without revealing her identity. He then meets Alphaeus, the river god, and the nymph, Arethusa; he prays for their happiness, and Arethusa, in the form of a stream, propels him upwards until he sees the sea above his head. This signals the end of the first part of his journey.

Book 3 finds Endymion travelling across an ocean floor littered with wrecks and skeletons. His next encounter is with the sea god Glaucus, who has been turned into a terrifying and ancient man by the goddess Circe. He asks Endymion to perform the magic spell which will restore his original form and bring back his love, the nymph Scylla, whom Circe has transformed into a monster. Endymion obliges, and together they also reunite all the drowned lovers of years past. A celebration follows. Endymion swoons, and in a trance he receives a message that he will soon be rewarded for his devotion with an endless heaven of love. He awakens to find himself back on land.

Book 4 opens with Endymion, now ready to undertake his final journey, finding an Indian maid; she sings a song of sorrow and asks him for comfort. Endymion falls deeply in love with the Indian maid. Hermes, messenger of the gods, carries them sleeping up to heaven; Endymion finds Cynthia, goddess of the moon (also

**CONTEXT**

The sixteenth-century playwright, John Lyly, wrote a comedy *Endimion*, and long after Keats's death Benjamin Disraeli would write a novel, *Endymion*, about a reflective, kind-hearted boy who eventually becomes prime minister.

known as Diana), leaning over him and realises this is the woman of his dreams. He moves to embrace her and she vanishes, and so, too, does the Indian maid. In the Cave of Quietude, Endymion falls asleep, and awakens to find the Indian maid beside him. He gives up his hopeless love for the moon goddess for the sake of his human love. She, however, is unable to accept his invitation to share his life within the forest. He decides to become a hermit, and she to serve Diana/Cynthia, goddess of the moon and chastity. Eventually, the Indian maid is transformed before his eyes into the goddess of his dreams, and the poem ends with Cynthia and Endymion vanishing together.

## COMMENTARY

As this summary will suggest, *Endymion* is a poem crowded with events, full of digressions. There is a sense of progression but not progress; the plot suggests a delightful and leisurely wandering, and this is well served by the **couplets**, partly because they effectively confirm the sense of delay, and partly because, as they are frequently **run on** rather than **closed**, they simultaneously suggest movement. **Closure** is promised but constantly deferred, and pleasure comes from the invitation to linger and ponder upon the delicate and intricate details, the rich and sensuous descriptions. Many of the apparent digressions focus on the recreation of a lost pagan world. These include the much admired 'Hymn to Pan' in Book 1 (lines 232–306). Often considered the most successful passage in the poem, this has been seen as a precursor of the great odes. The worshippers call upon the god and plead to be allowed to transcend mere earthly life, for him to 'be still the leaven, / That spreading in this dull and clodded earth / Gives it a touch ethereal – a new birth' (Book 1, lines 296–8). Nevertheless, what they are celebrating is primarily physical rather than spiritual nature, and the passage is notable for the way it evokes the simple sensual beauty of the pagan world. There is an accumulation of adjectives and even compound adjectives in such phrases as the 'Broad leaved fig trees', 'yellow girted bees', 'fairest blossom'd beans' and 'poppied corn' (Book 1, lines 252–7). Image is stacked upon image to create a sense of fertility and abundance. In this respect there is an implicit rejection of ascetic Christianity, with its focus on self-denial and its suspicion of the sensual life, in favour of pagan joy and amorality. Like many of the **Romantics**, Keats admired the ideals and

> **CONTEXT**
>
> Pan is the Greek god of shepherds and flocks and is responsible for their fertility. He has a human torso but the legs, ears and horns of a goat. According to legend, at the moment of Christ's Crucifixion, sailors on the coast of Greece heard a great voice shouting that Pan was dead: the pagan world dies with the beginnings of Christianity.

**CONTEXT**

Greece came under the domination of the Turkish Ottoman Empire in the fifteenth century. Following the revolt against Turkish rule in 1821 and the subsequent Greek War of Independence, Greece was established as an independent kingdom in 1833.

**CONTEXT**

Platonism consists of a complex body of ideas originating in the dialogues of the Greek philosopher Plato. In the context of Keats, most important is the idea that for Platonists earthly beauty hints at a more perfect ideal beauty.

achievements of classical Greece, and lamented its modern degradation under Turkish rule. When Wordsworth dismissed the 'Hymn to Pan' as a very pretty piece of Paganism, little more than decorative fancy, he was responding not only to the elaborate language which went against his own practice, but also to the **ideologically** charged nature of the passage, the implicit attack upon the Christian code (see **Literary background**).

Early critics often read this long poem as an **allegorical** rendering of the traditional Platonic ascent from sensual to spiritual love. Endymion's quest is, in this reading, equated with the soul's yearning for and eventual attainment of ideal beauty and immortality. Other critics countered that the spiritual aspirations of the poem were conveyed far less convincingly than its sensual eroticism, and argued for *Endymion* as a celebration of sexual love. Most critics now consider that the poem actually demonstrates the interconnectedness of the sensual and the spiritual, and that to emphasise one over the other is to distort the meaning of the poem. The spiritual ideal is only attainable through, and is inseparable from, individual sensual experience. The main theme, in this reading, becomes the need to accept the actual physical world of the senses before the spiritual can be known and appreciated. Endymion wins the divine goddess of the moon, but only after he chooses the Indian maid, a mortal woman.

The narrative quest for the visionary woman is a key pattern in the poems of Keats, and it is useful to consider how the questing male and the visionary female in *Endymion* anticipate or contrast with similar later figures in poems like 'La Belle Dame sans Merci', 'Lamia', or 'The Fall of Hyperion'. Another of the Romantics who draws upon the male quest for the visionary woman is Shelley. Endymion's rejection of the apparently unattainable goddess in favour of the Indian maid contrasts strikingly with the choice made by Shelley's visionary quester in *Alastor*. He pays much less attention to his devoted Arab maiden and forges ahead with the futile search for his ideal. Endymion's rejection of dream for reality is an affirmation of humanity, a recognition that the ideal can only be attained through the real (see **Themes**, on **A life of sensations**).

Some critics, disturbed by what they see as a somewhat abrupt and awkward ending, have suggested that since Endymion ultimately achieves his dream ideal this early poem goes against the pattern usually found in the later poems. More characteristically in Keats, the mortal enters some immortal dream land only to awaken back in the world of cold reality. There is no such disillusion in *Endymion*, no such ironic distancing as is found in, for example, 'Ode to a Nightingale' or 'La Belle Dame sans Merci'. How can the ending be reconciled with those passages in the poem which seem to caution against visionary yearning and assert the deceptiveness of transcendent experience? 'I have clung / To nothing, lov'd a nothing', Endymion declares when he decides to relinquish his quest for the divine and choose the Indian maid, 'I have been / Presumptuous against love' (Book 4, lines 636–9).

A key passage in Book 1 that has been drawn upon to support both the Platonic and sensual readings is that generally referred to as 'The Pleasure Thermometer' (lines 777–842). Keats wrote to his publisher, John Taylor, that he felt when writing this passage, 'a regular stepping of the Imagination towards a Truth'. Having written that argument, he continued, 'will perhaps be of the greatest service to me of anything I ever did. It set before me at once the gradations of happiness even like a kind of Pleasure Thermometer' (*Letters* 1, p. 218). The speech, spoken by Endymion to his sister Peona when she challenges the validity of his dream, measures degrees of happiness with reference to its intensity and selfless involvement. 'Wherein lies happiness?' he asks, and provides his own answer:

> … In that which becks
> Our ready minds to fellowship divine,
> A fellowship with essence; till we shine
> Full alchemiz'd, and free of space.
> Behold The clear religion of heaven!
>
> (Book 1, lines 777–81)

What does Keats mean here by 'essence'? Traditionally critics have provided either a Platonic interpretation with essence as the ideal or an anti-Platonic reading with essence as an earthly thing of beauty. Later critics have noted that the key to the passage is probably the

---

**CONTEXT**

Percy Bysshe Shelley composed his poem *Alastor* (meaning 'the evil spirit or demon of solitude') in 1815 and it was published in 1816. In it the hero abandons an 'Arab maiden' and travels through 'Arabie' and Persia, finally dying alone and unfulfilled in the 'Indian Caucasus'.

word 'alchemiz'd' and its relationship to chemical theory
(remember Keats's medical training). Human beings are changed or
'alchemiz'd' by blending with nature or with other beings. They
achieve a 'sort of oneness' (Book 1, line 796), a pleasurable 'self-
destroying' enthralment (Book 1, line 799). As in chemistry the
purest distillate or essence is created by the greatest intensity of
heat, so the most intense pleasure is the purest. The four 'degrees'
on the 'thermometer' coincide with the happiness provided by
nature, music, friendship and love. At the lower degrees are the feel
of a rose leaf and the sounds of music; at the higher degrees, the
'chief intensity' is 'made of love and friendship' (Book 1, lines
800–1). Even these, however, can be separated by further
distillation: the 'more ponderous and bulky worth' of friendship is
separated from the 'orbèd drop / Of light' that is love. And it is this
purest distillate or essence that produces the most intense happiness,
the most intense experience of blending and mingling. This does
not, of course, completely answer the question of what kind of love
Endymion is referring to. Is it necessary for us to choose one over
the other?

While critical readings of *Endymion* have frequently focused on the
question of love, it has also been read as an allegorical quest
narrative depicting the poet's search for true imaginative powers and
the series of tests and initiation rites that must be undergone before
this can be achieved. Such a reading is inevitably linked to the
reading which focuses on love since the imagination, like human
love, is seen capable of providing access to immortal truth. As
Endymion must accept earthly love in order to access the divine, so
the poet's imagination must accept and work on the physical world,
on the world of the senses, in order to discover a transcendent
world. In this respect *Endymion* may be seen as a poetic rendering
of Keats's declaration in a letter to Benjamin Bailey: 'The
Imagination may be compared to Adam's dream – he awoke and
found it truth.' (*Letters* 1, p. 185). As Adam dreams of the creation
of Eve and awakens to find her present, so the visionary imagination
can be prophetic, can shadow forth some essential truth (see
**Themes**, on **Imagination and transcendence**).

It is beyond the scope of these Notes to provide a glossary for this
4,000-line poem.

## ON SITTING DOWN TO READ KING LEAR ONCE AGAIN 1818 (1838)

- The poet addresses Romance personified.
- The poet turns away from romance in favour of tragedy.

**CHECK THE BOOK**

*King Lear*, Shakespeare's tragic drama, was written 1604–5 and based on an episode from Holinshed's *Chronicles*, which in turn was taken from Geoffrey of Monmouth's *Historia Britonum* of the twelfth century. In it the legendary king of England divides his kingdom between two of his daughters, disinheriting his third more honest daughter Cordelia. The two daughters harass him into madness, and when Cordelia rallies an army to dethrone her sisters, she is killed. Lear dies of grief over her body.

The poet bids farewell to seductive romance. He shuts these pages and plans to immerse himself again in the tragedy of Shakespeare's *King Lear*. By leaving behind the naïve and escapist mode of romance and submitting himself to the fire of tragic human experience as embodied by *Lear* he hopes to emerge poetically renewed.

## COMMENTARY

The sonnet begins with an apostrophe to a personified Romance. She is addressed as 'golden-tongued', a 'Syren', and 'Queen of far-away' (lines 1–2). While Keats finds her attractive and seductive, he also recognises her dangers and limitations. Why is Romance feminised? Keep in mind that the term 'Romance' seems to refer here not only to a literary genre but to a type of experience or perception marked by its unreal serenity and its remoteness from the everyday world of strife and action (see **Themes**, on **Romance**). Another mode of perception is required in order for Keats to participate fully in the English poetic tradition represented by Shakespeare. Without an awareness of the tragic nature of the human condition, the poet only wanders in some 'barren dream' (line 12). **Metaphorically** drawing upon the myth of the phoenix, Keats describes how he must submit himself to the fire of experience as embodied in such tragedies as *King Lear* in order that he may be poetically renewed. Is there any reluctance in Keats's decision to turn to tragedy? The use of the word 'Must' (line 7) implies that he is compelled to do this. Why is this tragic poetry more appropriate for a 'wintry day' (line 3)?

Some critics who see the repudiation of romance and of the reality of visionary experience as a central theme in Keats's work point to this sonnet as the turning point after which Keats regarded romance with an increasingly sceptical eye. After this, they believe, he was an antiromantic. Other critics, however, consider that there is a continuing struggle with romance throughout his poetry, and that he never manages to reconcile his romantic yearning for transcendence with his awareness of the harsh realities of the human condition exposed by history.

Keats effectively uses the formal divisions inherent in the sonnet form to structure his developing thought. While it primarily follows the Petrarchan form, the sonnet concludes with the couplet typical of the Shakespearean sonnet, anticipating Keats's move to the Shakespearean form in 'When I have fears' (see **Poetic form** and **Versification**). Given the movement in Keats's thought here from romance to tragedy, this is particularly appropriate. Another innovation is the lengthened final line, which breaks with the previous pattern of pentameters (lines with five feet). How does this formally enact the desire expressed in this final line?

> **CONTEXT**
>
> Francesco Petrarca, known as Petrarch, was a fourteenth-century Italian poet, who came from Tuscany, spent much of his adult life in exile in Avignon, returning finally to Italy when he was in his late forties. In Provence he fell in love with Laura and the style of his sonnets to her were subsequently much imitated and translated by English poets such as Thomas Wyatt, the Earl of Surrey, Thomas Watson, Sir Philip Sidney, Drummond of Hawthornden, Henry Parker, Lord Morley and the Countess of Pembroke.

> **GLOSSARY**
>
> 9   **Albion** an ancient name for Britain, the setting of *King Lear*
>
> 14  **Phoenix** this mythical bird which burned itself to ashes and emerges reborn suggests both the renewal of life and purification through fire

## WHEN I HAVE FEARS 1818 (1848)

- The poet expresses his fears that death will deny him fulfilment.

The first quatrain expresses the poet's fears that he may die before he has written all the poems he wants to. This is expanded upon in the second quatrain with a more specific reference to the possibility he may never trace all the 'high romance' he sees symbolised in the heavens. In the third quatrain he addresses a woman whom he met in a brief encounter to consider that he may also be prevented from ever experiencing love. Finally, he presents an image of himself standing alone on the shore of the wide world with all personal ambitions and concerns erased from his mind by the immensity of what he contemplates.

## COMMENTARY

'When I have fears' clearly demonstrates Shakespeare's influence upon Keats. To begin with, this is Keats's first **Shakespearean sonnet**, and he follows the requirements of the form quite closely. The lines are **end-stopped**, and the ideas developed accord with the divisions offered by the three quatrains; the repetition of such opening words as 'When' or 'And when' both link and simultaneously emphasise the divisions of the quatrains. The way in which the sense of the concluding couplet spills back to the last quatrain effectively undermines the epigrammatic tendency of the regular form which Keats considered to have a potentially trivialising effect. In addition, the Shakespearean influence is felt in the subject matter. Shakespearean sonnets about the destructiveness of Time that are useful for comparison include 'When I have seen by Time's fell hand defaced' and 'Like as the waves make towards the pebbled shore'.

Keats uses numerous natural images to describe the process of composition. He compares his fertile 'teeming' (line 2) brain to a field of corn: the act of writing is the reaping of the harvest, something he fears he may not live to complete; his books are the barns in which the grain is stored. Abstract ideas are repeatedly transformed into concrete and highly pictorial images. It has been suggested that this sonnet is actually more concerned with self-doubt, with the threat of failure as a poet, rather than with the threat of early death which Keats so prophetically describes. Is there any evidence to support this argument? While Keats may create a sense of fulfilment through the natural imagery described above, he also creates a sense of disappointment, a sense of individual insignificance. The lightness suggested by the lines describing the 'fair creature of an hour' (line 9) is succeeded by a sense of heaviness. How are these contrasting effects achieved? What does Keats see or recognise as he stands alone on the shore of the wide world that drives all thoughts of love and fame, all personal concerns, from his head?

 **CHECK THE NET**

For an online version of Keats's poems, look at Great books on line:**http.//www. bartleby.com/ people/Keats-Jo. html.**

**GLOSSARY**

| | |
|---|---|
| 3 | charact'ry writing |

## ISABELLA; OR THE POT OF BASIL 1818 (1820)

- Isabella's lover Lorenzo is murdered by her brothers.
- His ghost appears to her and reveals his fate.
- She digs up the body, cuts off the head, and puts it in a pot of basil.
- The brothers steal the pot and Isabella dies of a broken heart.

**CHECK THE NET**

Giovanni Boccaccio's *Decameron* is a classic in Italian medieval literature, and provides a rich portrayal of life in mid fourteenth-century Florence. Further information can be found on the Decameron website, which includes a section on Romantic retellings of the tales:

**http://www.brown. edu/Departments/ Italian_Studies/ dweb/search/index. shtml.**

**CHECK THE BOOK**

For a complete critical reading of 'Isabella' see: Jack Stillinger, 'Keats and Romance', in *Studies in English Literature, 1500–1900*, **8** (1968), pp. 593–605.

In this verse rendition of a tale which he found in Boccaccio's *Decameron*, Keats relates the story of Isabella and Lorenzo. Isabella's two proud and ambitious brothers, who have always planned for their sister to marry someone of great wealth and property, disapprove of the humble Lorenzo. They lure him away, murder him, and bury his body in a forest, telling Isabella he has had to leave the country. Isabella is desolate when she does not hear from Lorenzo. One night, his ghost appears to her, revealing his fate and telling her where his body can be found. Isabella goes there with her old nurse, disinters her lover and removes his head. She then places the head within a garden pot and covers it with a plant of sweet basil. Watered by her tears, the basil thrives wonderfully. Her brothers, guilt-stricken, have meanwhile been tormented by nightmares. Observing how she cherishes this pot, they steal it, discover the head, and rush from Florence in terror. Isabella mourns her new loss, pines away, and dies, 'Imploring for her Basil to the last' (line 498). The memory of her love and suffering is immortalised in the Florentine community as a song based on her words.

## COMMENTARY

A plot summary of this gruesome tale inevitably diminishes the poem and tends to suggest Keats was right in thinking it 'too smokeable' (*Letters* 2, p. 174), that is, too vulnerable to ridicule. The poem was extremely popular throughout much of the nineteenth century, particularly with the Pre-Raphaelites (you might want to look at Millais's *Isabella* and Holman Hunt's *Isabella and the Pot of Basil*). It has, however, been disliked by many twentieth-century critics, and only quite recently become considered worthy of reconsideration. The poem is now of interest to many contemporary critics who see Romanticism as dialectic, depending upon the interplay of contradictions and oppositions, rather than, as was traditionally thought by many formalists, synthetic, fusing and reconciling oppositions. As a text which invites the reader to speculate about various potential readings, 'Isabella' is now valued far more than it was, an interesting indication of how literary canons change as critics look for and value different features.

For 'Isabella', Keats appropriately chose to write in *ottava rima*, a stanzaic form originally created by Boccaccio during the fourteenth century. In these eight-line stanzas of **iambic pentameter** with the rhyme scheme *abababcc*, the alternately rhymed first six lines seem to build up with a 'punch line' effect in the concluding couplet. But Keats, after choosing a stanzaic form which suggests resolution through that couplet, repeatedly leaves stanzas open, promising but withholding conclusions. The rhyme in this poem has in the past been dismissed as clumsy and pretentious; stanza 24 provides an example of what critics have objected to with the somewhat laboured rhymes of 'Apennine', 'eglantine' and 'whine' (lines 186, 188, 190). However, in rejecting the smooth polish and elegance of the eighteenth-century couplet in favour of rougher, more primitive rhymes, Keats can in fact be seen as quite innovative, matching the primitive medieval world with appropriate rhetoric. The verse form produces a highly stylised mood, and this mood is emphasised by the frequent use of **antithesis** and repetition.

The narrator's tone sometimes appears comically inappropriate for such a grisly tale: 'Ah, wherefore all this wormy circumstance' (line 385) he comments when the corpse is disinterred. The narrator also seems, at times, ironically distanced from romance conventions; this may be a romance, but he warns the reader against wasting tears on the lovers. Then, in apparent contradiction of this ironic stance, while he graphically renders all the gruesome details of death and dismemberment, he also expresses a longing for the gentleness of old romance. The narrator is obtrusive and self-conscious, frequently drawing our attention to the fact that he is telling a story; this is a form of **Romantic irony**. He often turns to address Boccaccio, for example, asking 'forgiving boon' (line 146) for appropriating his work. Indeed, the poem is often considered to be more interested in its digressions than in its main gruesome

---

**CONTEXT**

Keats's contemporary, the essayist Charles Lamb (1775-1834) thought that *Isabella* was the best of Keats's poems published in *Lamia, Isabella, Eve of St Agnes and Other Poems* (1820), but Keats grew to dislike it intensely.

narrative. One of the most successful passages, for example, is concerned not with the main theme of disappointed love but with the 'money-mongering' of Isabella's brothers (stanzas 14–17). This is a strikingly angry passage, full of high rhetoric: 'Why were they proud?' he says of Isabella's brothers, 'again we ask aloud, / Why in the name of Glory were they proud' (lines 127–8). Why is Keats so interested in the brothers' pride and greed? He may be making the old tale, the 'gentleness of old Romance' (line 387) more relevant to nineteenth-century readers by criticising a capitalistic society; he may be introducing ironic distance by suggesting the materialism that underlies idealistic romance.

One standard way of reading 'Isabella' is to see it encapsulating an opposition which is often considered central to and typical of Keats's poetry: the opposition between the worlds of romantic enchantment and cold reality. Young love, sexual passion, sensual richness and idealism are set against heartless capitalism and rational empiricism: the rich life of the senses and imagination against the poverty of everyday experience. The first set of terms in this series of oppositions is represented by the young lovers, and the second by the two brothers who destroy their idyllic world. To read the poem this way might lead us to interpret such episodes as the visit of Lorenzo's ghost and Isabella's exhumation of her lover's body and strange cultivation of his head as a lament for the loss of love and pleasure and beauty which results from the pressures of social and economic demands, the expression of a poignant longing to escape reality (see **Themes**).

One might counter, however, that the poem sometimes resists the simple good/bad opposition suggested by such a reading. Supposedly oppositional terms repeatedly become intermingled; notions of beauty, for example, are intricately involved in scenes of horror. The idealistic world of the lovers can be considered just as limited as the brothers' cold, rational world. Absorbed in their passion, Lorenzo and Isabella exclude the larger world of human society. In this sense their naïveté and complete unawareness of the outside world make them vulnerable, unable to cope with or defend themselves against the manipulative tactics of the more worldly brothers. In this sense, we might see the poem as actually questioning the feasibility of their idealism.

A psychoanalytical reading might focus upon what the poem is suggesting about the construction of identity. Because of Lorenzo's reticence, the lovers' desire to tell their love is repeatedly deferred and displaced. Isabella can find no identity through love and is only defined as female when the passion between the lovers is transformed through death into a mother-child relationship. Lorenzo's head in the pot becomes the macabre object of a 'child' which Isabella, in a perverse maternal role, nurtures with her tears. A Marxist-feminist reading of 'Isabella' might instead suggest that the identities of both Lorenzo and Isabella are actually defined through love, but that they accept, and subordinate their emotions to, social codes of sexual behaviour. Lorenzo plays the courtly lover, and Isabella the modest and passive object of his love. These roles, a Marxist would point out, have been established to serve the economic interests of society.

**WWW. CHECK THE NET**

Both John Everett Millais and William Holman Hunt illustrate passages from Keats' 'Isabella'. See http://www.abcgallery.com/liter/keats.html.

---

**GLOSSARY**

| | |
|---|---|
| 95 | **Theseus' spouse** Ariadne, deserted on an island by Theseus after she had helped him defeat the Minotaur |
| 99 | **Dido** Queen of Carthage. According to Virgil's *Aeneid*, she killed herself for love of Aeneas after he abandoned her |
| 132 | **Paled in** enclosed |
| 140 | **Egypt's pest** swarms of flies. Exodus 8:21 |
| 150 | **ghittern** guitar |
| 262 | **Hinnom's vale** where Ahaz burnt his children as a sacrifice to Moloch (II Chronicles 28:3) |
| 393 | **Perséan sword** Perseus cut off the head of the Gorgon Medusa with his sword |
| 435 | **Lethean** Lethe is one of the rivers of Hades; the dead are obliged to drink from it in order that they may forget everything said and done when alive |
| 442 | **Melpomene** muse of tragedy |
| 451 | **Baälites of pelf** worshippers of money, like pagans who sacrificed to Baäl |

## HYPERION: A FRAGMENT 1818 (1820)

- The Titans, usurped by the new Olympian gods, mourn their lost empire.
- The still unfallen Hyperion continues to struggle, but must eventually accept defeat.
- He is replaced by Apollo, whose emergence into godhead is presided over by Mnemosyne.

This unfinished poem in three books is based on the Greek myth of the defeat of the Titans. Under Saturn, the Titans, including Hyperion, a sun god, ruled the universe. They were overthrown by the Olympians, led by three sons of Saturn: Jupiter, Neptune and Pluto. Hyperion was replaced by Apollo, who was also a sun god but had, in addition, particular associations with music and poetry. Keats sees in the myth a means to express faith in the idea of progress. Even the old gods must admit that their successors are more beautiful and therefore better fitted to rule.

Book 1 opens *in media res* with the deposed god Saturn mourning the loss of his empire to Jupiter. Thea, another of the Titans and sister/wife to Hyperion, attempts to comfort him, but, also despairing, she can only weep at his feet. Saturn rouses himself to renewed resistance and is led by Thea to where the other fallen Titans are assembled. The second part of Book 1 focuses on Hyperion, still unvanquished and defiant but apprehensive and suffering from premonitions of death and disaster, preparing to go to the aid of Saturn.

Book 2 describes the council of the deposed Titans, as they attempt to come to terms with their new powerlessness. Saturn arrives, guided by Thea, and opens the debate. The speech given by Oceanus is the most positive: he urges his fellow Titans to come to terms with change as an inevitable part of the natural process, and ends by praising the beauty of his own supplanter, the new god of the seas, Neptune. Clymene, a sea nymph, supports Oceanus. Her lament declares the uselessness of philosophical arguments in dispelling grief, but also confirms Oceanus's wisdom when she

### CONTEXT

This unfinished poem was written very much in the style of John Milton (1608-74). Many of Milton's poems were written in Latin, but his most famous epic poems, *Paradise Lost* and *Paradise Regained*, were still very popular throughout the nineteenth century.

describes the beautiful music with which the earth greeted the arrival of Apollo, the new god of song. Enceladus does not agree and urges them all to challenge the enemy, reminding them that Hyperion is still unfallen. Hyperion himself arrives, but he has now accepted defeat.

The brief, fragmentary Book 3 describes the valley where Apollo, who will be the new sun god, is coming into his powers. Mnemosyne, herself a Titan, the goddess of memory and mother of the nine Muses, presides over the initiation ceremony. Apollo, whose poetic associations are emphasised by his possession of a lyre, reads a 'wondrous lesson' (Book 3, line 112) in her face, and 'Knowledge enormous' (Book 3, line 113) transforms him into a god. Book 3 breaks off with his assumption of godhead.

## COMMENTARY

*Hyperion* invites comparisons with *Paradise Lost* by presenting another epic version of the Fall in Miltonic blank verse. Similarities can be seen in both the epic theme and the structure – including the opening *in media res*, with the Titans already fallen – and in specific scenes: the council of the defeated Titans in Book 1, for example, echoes Milton's description of the fallen angels in Hell. But while Milton is concerned with the fall and redemption of humankind, Keats is more interested in a cyclic process of improvement prompted by aesthetic vision, the replacement of a somewhat rigid divine dispensation by a more natural and humane order.

Compare the style of *Hyperion* with the earlier *Endymion*, and consider how the new leaner, harder language is more appropriate for Keats's engagement with the world of power struggles. The luxuriant diction and pleasurable sense of wandering in *Endymion* is replaced by terse and disciplined language in *Hyperion*, by grand and forceful diction, an emphatic sense of action, of movement towards a particular climactic moment. Numerous action verbs drive the narrative onwards, suggesting the relentless movement from old to new order, from Hyperion to Apollo.

Compare the way in which these old and new orders are represented. Analyse the effect of the numerous negatives and the emphasis on deathly silence and stillness with which *Hyperion*

> **CONTEXT**
>
> Why Keats never finished writing either *Hyperion* or its recast version 'The Fall of Hyperion' is not known, but he did imply in a letter to his friend John Hamilton Reynolds that he thought it too Miltonic.

**CONTEXT**

Epics are long narrative poems written in an elevated style about the exploits of superhuman heroes. The earliest example is the Sumerian epic Gilgamesh (c. 2700 BC). Classical examples include the *Odyssey* and the *Iliad* (c. 8th century BC) traditionally ascribed to Homer.

begins. How often, throughout the poem, are negatives and stillness associated with the Titans? Although the poem is generally written in lofty and grave verse, there is an abrupt change in the tone at the beginning of Book 3 with the introduction of Apollo. Epic stateliness is replaced with a return to the lusher style and imagery of *Endymion*. The contrast between the old gods and the new is emphasised by the differences in landscape and style between the austere scene where the Titans gather in Book 2 and the valley in which Apollo becomes immortal in Book 3. The dark, craggy, barren landscape and the sonorous, weighty cadences of the former are replaced by a luxuriant, sensuous, glowing world and much lighter, lilting rhythms before the more measured, grander style returns with Apollo's assumption of godhead.

The poem is full of images of measure, increase and diminishment, rising and falling. Keats uses, for example, varying intensities of light to suggest dynastic revolution. What happens to the radiance and brilliance of the 'bright Titan' (Book 1, line 299) Hyperion? What are the main changes in the world now the Olympians are in ascendance? It has been said that *Hyperion* is both a gigantic elegy and a hymn to the future, that although Keats is primarily concerned with evolutionary progress, his sympathies are still engaged by the spectacle of fallen greatness. Is there any specific evidence that the poem is both elegiac and forward looking?

*Hyperion* has also been described as a poem which seeks to assert the authority of a poet and explores the role of the poet in relation to history. How is Apollo associated with poetic power and in what way does he become a type of the negatively capable poet (see **Themes**, on **Negative capability**)? What is the lesson he reads in Mnemosyne's face? It is through 'knowledge enormous' that Apollo becomes a god, and this knowledge seems to be primarily of suffering. How might the acquisition of such knowledge be related to both a widened and deepened human consciousness and to poetic power? If Apollo represents some kind of new creative force, why is Saturn now rendered impotent? 'But cannot I create? / Cannot I form?' (Book 1, lines 141–2).

This unfinished epic was later recast in the form of a dream vision, 'The Fall of Hyperion'. Suggestions for comparisons between the two poems are offered in the notes on the later poem.

## GLOSSARY

**BOOK 1**

| | |
|---|---|
| 23 | **came one** Thea, a Titan, and Hyperion's sister and wife |
| 30 | **Ixion's wheel** Ixion was bound to a perpetually turning wheel for daring to make love to Juno |
| 31 | **Memphian** Memphis, ancient capital of Lower Egypt, near the sphinx and the pyramids |
| 147 | **rebel three** Jupiter, Pluto and Neptune, the three sons who overthrew their father Saturn |
| 171 | **gloom-bird** owl |
| 181 | **Aurorian** Aurora is the goddess of dawn |
| 207 | **Zephyrs** western breezes |
| 246 | **Tellus** goddess of the Earth |
| 274 | **colure** one of two intersecting circles in the celestial sphere |
| 307 | **Cœlus** Uranus, the sky |

**BOOK 2**

| | |
|---|---|
| 4 | **Cybele** wife of Saturn and mother of the Olympian gods |
| 19-20 | **Cœs ... Porphyrion** various giants and Titans |
| 28 | **gurge** whirlpool |
| 29 | **Mnemosyne** goddess of memory and mother of the Muses |
| 30 | **Phœbe** goddess of the moon |
| 41 | **Creüs** a Titan, divinity of the sea |
| 44 | **Iäpetus** a Titan, father of Prometheus |
| 49 | **Cottus** one of the hundred-handed giants |
| 53 | **Asia** daughter of Oceanus and Tethys |
| 66 | **Enceladus** one of the hundred-handed giants and a leader in the war of the Giants against the Olympian gods |
| 75 | **Oceanus** the eldest Titan |
| 75 | **Tethys** wife of Oceanus |
| 76 | **Clymene** daughter of Oceanus and mother of Prometheus |
| 77 | **Themis** daughter of Saturn and mother of the Fates |
| 232 | **young God of the Seas** Neptune |
| 244 | **poz'd** puzzled |
| 376 | **Memnon's ... harp** according to tradition, the colossal statue of the Egyptian Memnon, near the Valley of Kings, uttered a mournful cry when struck by the rays of the rising sun |

**BOOK 3**

| | |
|---|---|
| 13 | **Father of all verse** Apollo |
| 29 | **Giant of the Sun** Hyperion |

## CONTEXT

The god Apollo embodied male beauty and moral excellence, and was associated with the beneficent aspects of civilisation. He gave to Greek culture the ideal of the beautiful, athletic and virtuous young man.

## THE EVE OF ST AGNES 1818 (1820)

- After the feast on St Agnes' Eve, Madeline prepares to dream of her future lover.
- Porphyro steals into her bedroom and hides.
- As she dreams he awakens her and she sees him in a living dream.
- Porphyro elopes with Madeline on St Agnes' Eve.

### CONTEXT

St Agnes is the patron saint of young virgins, possibly martyred in the Diocletian persecution (c.304) at the age of thirteen; she vowed that her body be consecrated to Christ and rejected all her suitors. According to legend, virgins may see their future husbands in their dreams during the night of St Agnes' Eve (20 January).

It is the eve of St Agnes, and a bitterly cold night. An ancient pensioner returns from his prayers through an empty chapel. He hears the sound of music coming from the castle above but continues on his way to say prayers for the souls of sinners. In the castle, preparations for the celebratory feast held on St Agnes's Eve are completed and the guests arrive. The narrator turns away from them to focus on Madeline who, oblivious to the guests and music, is thinking only of the legend of St Agnes. Virgins who observe certain ceremonial rites on this particular eve may see their future husbands in their dreams. Meanwhile Porphyro approaches the castle; he is in love with Madeline, but their fathers are sworn enemies. He penetrates the castle and learns from Angela, the aging nurse, that Madeline is performing the rites associated with St Agnes. Angela reluctantly agrees to help Porphyro conceal himself in Madeline's bedchamber and then brings a selection of delicacies from the feast. Porphyro watches Madeline prepare for bed and fall asleep and then arranges the delicacies on a table. He tries but fails to awaken her. Eventually, playing her lute, he arouses her from dreams of him to a state between sleeping and waking in which she confesses her love; at this point, 'Into her dream he melted' (line 320). Their relationship is consummated as a storm arises, and Madeline is fully awakened. Initially distressed and fearing he will now forsake her, she eventually consents to elope with her lover and the two steal out of the castle under cover of the storm which now rages outside. The poem concludes with a reminder from the narrator that this all happened long ago.

## COMMENTARY

'The Eve of St Agnes' is a narrative poem in which the narrative impulse repeatedly leads towards description. The poem is primarily notable for its elaborate pictorial and musical effects. Its wealth of description meant that, like 'Isabella', the poem became a favourite with the Pre-Raphaelite artists of the nineteenth century. (You might look, for example, at Maclise's *Madeline after Prayer* or Hunt's *Flight of Madeline and Porphyro* and *Eve of St Agnes*.) Keats's use of the Spenserian stanza formally encourages this tendency towards descriptiveness. The stanza, containing eight lines of iambic pentameter and a final alexandrine, a line of iambic hexameter, does not require the kind of compression associated with the *ottava rima* Keats used in 'Isabella'. Nevertheless, as a self-contained unit, it encourages the creation of tableaux.

 **CHECK THE NET**
See Daniel Maclise's *Madeline after Prayer* at http://www.artmagick.com/images/paintings01/maclise/maclise1.jpg.

The poem is also notable for its varied and sensual **imagery** and **synaesthetic** richness. There is, for example, the imagery of sculpture used to suggest the way feeling is arrested or repressed and then released. There is a linked series of musical themes and images at work in the poem; in light of what has been said about sculpture, what is the significance of the image of the ballroom filled with 'music, yearning like a God in pain' (line 56). What use does Keats make of colour imagery? What are the effects of the numerous animals, birds and insects in the poem? Many images in this poem function to suggest opposition and set up boundaries: the cold outside is set against the warmth within, the noise and revelry of the feasters in the castle against the calm and quiet of Madeline's room, and the snarling trumpets which welcome the guests against the tender chords of the lute.

The poem has also been much admired for its dramatic immediacy. This is partly achieved by the way the tense fluctuates between past and present, one more of the oppositions that the poem sets up. In stanza 22, for example, there is a movement from past to present when the narrator, reflecting a sense of rising excitement, turns from straight description to address the concealed Porphyro, alerting him to the arrival of Madeline: 'Now prepare, / Young Porphyro, for gazing on that bed; / She comes, she comes again, like ring-dove fray'd and fled' (lines 196–8). Following this, there is a return to the past tense until Madeline starts undressing when, again, we move into the more dramatic present tense in stanza 26. The narrative also moves into the present when the lovers make their escape, suggesting a sense of haste and urgency. While we have been caught

**CHECK THE BOOK**

For a detailed study of the complexities of writing, reading and interpretation with particular reference to 'The Eve of St Agnes', see Jack Stillinger, *Reading the Eve of St. Agnes: The Multiples of Complex Literary Transaction.* Oxford, Oxford U.P., 1999.

up in the sensual immediacy of Porphyro and Madeline, we are now reminded that this all happened long ago, that we live in quite a different world. The concluding stanza might be seen to puncture the world of make-believe, distancing us from events, but perhaps this distance has always been subtly maintained throughout the poem by the narrator's tone, creating a tension between scepticism and the will to believe, between dream and reality.

Thematically, too, the poem can be seen as structured around a series of oppositions, and one of the most central of these is this opposition between dream and reality. The world of the young lovers might be thought of as a dream world, a world where a rose may shut 'and be a bud again' (line 243). But, as we are often reminded, they actually live in a world where roses can only wither and die. If their love is to be validated, they must leave the protection of the warm and magical dream room and go out to face the storm. This reading of the opposition between dream and reality places both lovers initially on the side of dream.

There is, however, a great deal of evidence to suggest that the association of Porphyro with dreams is problematic from the start. Madeline desires a vision of her lover and a dream of consummation. Porphyro desires to gaze upon the actual form of Madeline and, perhaps, even to experience a physical consummation. Porphyro certainly gets what he wants, but are the two distinct desires resolved? Do *both* lovers get the fulfilment they crave or just Porphyro? Is the poem a celebration or an ironic critique of idealistic young love? Answering these questions involves making a decision about Porphyro's intentions. Does Porphyro intend to seduce Madeline all along; is that the thought which comes to him 'like a full-blown rose' (line 136)? In an influential essay entitled 'The Hoodwinking of Madeline', Jack Stillinger argues that Porphyro gains Madeline's bed only by a stratagem, a word used in the poem. Is Madeline then simply the victim of a trick? Do her dreams deceive her?

How we answer this question has significant implications for how we read the poem's position on the imagination. If he is bent on seduction from the start, Porphyro is villain as much as hero; the imagination, represented here by Madeline's dreams, is deceptive;

she is the deluded victim. Such a reading emphasises the latent ironies of the poem and presents it as a sceptical antiromance. It is possible, however, that Porphyro only intends to awaken her in order to ensure, in accordance with the legend, that he will become her husband: he goes into the room with no plan, as Keats delicately puts it, to melt into her dream. If this is the case, the poem would seem to affirm the powers of romance and the imagination. His imaginative stratagem works; Madeline's dream comes true; the desires of both are fulfilled. Evidence can be found to support both sides of the argument; Madeline's dream does come true, but what makes it come true is a trick. Is the power of the imagination then both affirmed *and* ironically subverted (see **Themes**, on **Imagination and transcendence**)?

**QUESTION**

Are we to condemn Porphyro's behaviour in 'The Eve of St Agnes' or not?

---

**GLOSSARY**

71   **St Agnes … lambs**  on St Agnes's day two lambs were offered at the altar

126   **mickle**  much

171   **Merlin … demon**  According to Arthurian legend, the wizard Merlin was the son of a demon

174   **tambour frame**  embroidery frame shaped like a drum

241   **Clasp'd … pray**  kept shut as a Christian prayer book would be among the pagans

257   **Morphean**  Morpheus is the god of sleep

292   **La belle dame sans mercy**  poem by Alain Chartier, an early fifteenth-century French poet; see also Keats's poem of the same title

325   **flaw-blown**  wind blown

349   **Rhenish**  wine from the Rhine country

---

## BRIGHT STAR 1819 (1838)

- The poet addresses a star.
- He expresses a longing for permanence.

The poet addresses a star, expressing his longing to be as steadfast, but not on the same terms. The star is alone, it is sleepless and watches constantly and dispassionately the tides and seasons. Instead, the poet wishes to be as steadfast and unchangeable while pillowed upon his love's breast.

## COMMENTARY

This **Shakespearean sonnet** is traditionally associated with Fanny Brawne, who is assumed to be the 'fair love' of the **sestet** (set of six lines). It is constructed around the contrast of cold isolation and warm communion. The **octave** (set of eight lines) centres on the image of the bright star, traditionally an image of permanence. Shakespeare, for example, celebrates love as an 'ever-fixèd mark', the 'star to every wandering bark', in Sonnet 116. Keats develops the star as a symbol of perfection, of the steadfastness for which he longs. In this respect it may be usefully compared with such later similar images as the urn or the nightingale. It is fixed, remote, and passionless, far above the mortal world of flux. What does the language suggest is attractive about the star, and what are its limitations? What is the effect of the ascetic religious imagery?

The example of the star is rejected at the turn or **volta** with the word 'No'. Keats turns instead to the warmer erotic image of himself pillowed on his love's breast. As so often in Keats's work, he moves to seek immortality within the human condition, to find an enduring perfection rooted in the world of constant change. Does he achieve this? Consider the phrase 'sweet unrest' (line 12), and the thrice repeated 'ever'; are there any signs of ambivalence or contradiction here? It is possible that Keats recognises what he longs for is an impossibility, and that leads him to the alternative: 'or else swoon to death' (line 14). Death here may punningly suggest sexual climax, but the more literal meaning remains and this perhaps suggests the only way in which permanence can be achieved within the mortal world.

**CONTEXT**

Keats met Fanny Brawne (1800–65) in 1818. Financial difficulties and Keats's increasing health problems made their marriage impossible.

## ODE TO PSYCHE 1819 (1820)

- The poet invokes Psyche.
- He provides her with the temple and worship appropriate for a goddess.

The poet begins with an invocation to Psyche, apologising for singing to her of herself. He describes seeing the winged Cupid with Psyche in the forest. He laments that Psyche came to immortality too late to be treated in the manner of other gods, and asks that he be allowed to provide the worship she has not received. The final stanza presents him reflecting upon how he will fulfil his promise to provide her with a shrine and be her priest. He will create a haven for her in his own mind, and provide her with a fitting place in which to receive her beloved Cupid, god of love.

## COMMENTARY

According to myth, Psyche was a beautiful nymph loved by Cupid, god of love. He visited her each night, but departed at sunrise. Psyche was told never to attempt to discover his identity, but her curiosity won out. One night she lit a lamp by which to see him and some of the burning oil dropped upon him. Awakened and angry at being disobeyed, he left her. Psyche wandered in search of her lover and became the slave of Venus who imposed cruel tasks on her. Eventually she was reunited with Cupid and made immortal. Because of her late arrival on Olympus, as Keats observed, she was never honoured and worshipped in the way of the other gods.

This **ode** has often been seen as an extended **metaphor** about poetry, a reading that can be supported by an analysis of the development of ideas in relation to structure. Keats restores or recreates the forgotten Psyche twice in this poem, and these restorations occur within the two tableaux which frame the ode. When he asks 'Surely I dreamt to-day, or did I see / The winged Psyche with awaken'd eyes?' (lines 5–6) he introduces the first recreation. Here she is represented in a mythological past world, a forest bower, a place exterior to the passive poet's mind and accessible by dream or vision. The second recreation occurs when he vows to be her priest. Here she is more consciously and artfully recreated within the bower of the poet's mind and brought into the present (see **Themes**, on **Bowers**). The movement from one tableau to another is complemented by a change from the language of erotic experience to the language of aesthetic experience. Helen Vendler suggests this basic structure reveals how Keats envisions the function and process of art in this particular poem: it appears to be something completely internalised and mimetic, pure imaginative creation, the production of a mirror image.

> **CONTEXT**
>
> The story of Psyche and Cupid is told in books 4–6 of *Golden Ass*, a series of tales by Lucius Apuleius (c. AD 155).

Contrast the forest landscape of the opening tableau with the cultivated landscape created by the 'gardener Fancy' (line 62) in the closing tableau. The first lush natural setting is firmly anchored in sense impressions. Some critics have considered that by contrast the description in the final tableau is too consciously artful; is this true? How are the two deities represented in the opening? Are there any connections between them and the lover pictured on the later Grecian urn? Considering the urge towards duplication in this ode, it is significant that Keats's final stanza does not offer the figure of the two immortals embracing. If the final stanza offers Keats's view of poetic creation at this point, what has been lost? What has happened to the world of the senses and where is his audience?

> **? QUESTION**
> How does Keats use concrete nature images to describe mental processes in 'Ode to Psyche'?

Within the framework provided by these tableaux, Keats juxtaposes the nonexistent historical cult with the imagined mental cult that he, the poet, will provide. There is mirroring and duplication here too: the diction of negatives used to describe what Psyche has, historically, not been given, is replicated by the diction of affirmatives used to describe what he, the poet, will provide. What accounts for the change in tone between stanzas 2 and 3? Psyche, first addressed intimately as 'happy, happy dove'(line 22) is now provided with a formal series of lofty titles that emphasise her position as goddess. There is a movement from the warm language of physical love to the cooler language of religious formality. The highly ritualised stanzas 3 and 4 can be seen as Keats's Hymn to Psyche. What are the effects of the repeated rhetorical pattern, the use of **anaphora** and the symmetrical regularity of stanza 3? Consider some of the other rhetorical devices used in this ode. There is, for example, the **paradox** of 'tuneless numbers' (line 1) How is this device functional?

Psyche is not only a Greek goddess. She also represents the soul – Psyche being the Greek for breath and, therefore, for life or the soul itself – and is often represented as a butterfly. Some critics have seen this ode as an **allegory** of the soul, Keats's way of affirming that there is something godlike in the human soul which has not been recognised until modern times. Attempt an alternate reading of the ode with this allegory in mind.

| GLOSSARY | |
| --- | --- |
| 4 | conched  shell shaped |
| 14 | Tyrian  a purple dye made in Tyre |
| 26 | Phœbe's ... star  the moon |
| 41 | fans  wings |

## ODE TO A NIGHTINGALE 1819 (1820)

- In this meditation on poetic experience, the poet begins by describing his sadness.
- The poet attempts to conceptualise a reconciliation of beauty and permanence through the symbol of the nightingale.

**QUESTION**
'A question is the best beacon towards a little Speculation' said Keats (Letters 1: 175). What does the question with which 'Ode to a Nightingale' concludes encourage us to speculate about?

The poet begins by explaining the nature and cause of the sadness he is experiencing, a sadness translated into a physical ache and a drowsy numbness. He feels as he might if he had taken some poison or sedating drug. This feeling is in fact the result of a deep awareness of the happiness of the nightingale he hears singing. His resulting pleasure is so intense it has become painful. He longs for some intoxicant that will let him achieve union with the nightingale, take him out of the world, and allow him to forget human suffering and despair and the transience of all experience. Wine, however, is rejected in favour of the poetic imagination. He enters some twilight region of the mind. While he can see nothing, the other senses feed his imagination, constructing within his mind what cannot be seen in fact. This prompts him to contemplate leaving the world altogether. He realises, however, that the ultimate form of forgetfulness, of escape from the troubles of life, would be death. Death at such a moment, listening to the nightingale pouring forth its soul in ecstasy, would be the supreme ending. And yet death is rejected. As the poet realises, the bird would sing on, and he would be unable to hear it. While all humans must die, the nightingale is, in some sense, immortal. The poet, thinking back to the classical world of the Roman emperors and to the Old Testament world of Ruth, considers how its song has been heard for so many centuries. Keats takes us even further back, into a fairy

**CHECK
THE BOOK**

'It is disputed
whether the
Nightingale's song
should be
considered joyous or
melancholy. My own
opinion is that the
piteous wailing note
which is its most
characteristic nature,
casts a shade of
sadness over the
whole song, even
those portions
which gush with
the most exuberant
gladness...if the
Nightingale's song
comprised the
wailing notes alone,
it would be
universally shunned
as the most painfully
melancholy sound
in nature' - Rev.
C.A.Johns, *British
Birds in their Haunts*
(1909).

world, a landscape both magical and yet forlorn. With this word
'forlorn' (line 70), the spell is broken: the poet returns to the self, to
the present. Fancy, he claims, has failed him once more. He again
becomes aware of the landscape around him and the bird's song
begins to fade, leaving him wondering whether his experience was a
vision or a waking dream.

## COMMENTARY

The nightingale has traditionally been associated with love. The
influential myth of Philomela, turned into a nightingale after being
raped and tortured, stresses melancholy and suffering in association
with love. It has also been associated with poetry. Keats no doubt
knew Coleridge's two poems 'To the Nightingale' (1796) and 'The
Nightingale: "A Conversation Poem"', and, according to his letters,
only days before writing this ode he had talked with the older poet
on such subjects as nightingales, poetry and poetical sensation.

Why did Keats choose the nightingale's song as the basis of
meditation in this poem? Is he drawing upon its traditional
associations or not? Such critics as Helen Vendler believe that in the
choice of music Keats finds a symbol of pure beauty,
nonrepresentational, without any reference to ideas, to moral or
social values. The nightingale's song is vocal, but without verbal
content, and can serve as a pure expressive beauty. Other have
argued that it represents the music of nature, which can be
contrasted with human art, verbal or musical.

The poem is basically structured around the contrast between the
poet, who is earthbound, and the bird, which is free. A related
opposition is that between the mortal world, full of sorrow and
marked by transience, and the world of the nightingale, marked by
joy and immortality. One of the points that has troubled many
critics is this claim of immortality for the nightingale: 'Thou wast
not born for death, immortal Bird!' (line 61). The nightingale is,
after all, a natural creature. It has been suggested that Keats is
referring not to the individual bird, but to the species. This solution
has been strongly criticised, however, as humanity, the 'hungry
generations' (line 62), could also be credited with such immortality
as a species. An alternative suggestion is that the nightingale
addressed in stanza 7 is purely symbolic; is this solution more

convincing? If so, what does the nightingale symbolise? A further interpretation might be that, since the nightingale sings only at night and was traditionally thought of, therefore, as invisible, it, through its 'disembodied' song, transcends the material world (so in that sense is immortal); and here Keats is talking of 'embalmed darkness' (line 43), an atmosphere of death.

Another problematic point is Keats's final question on the status of his experience: 'Was it a vision, or a waking dream?' (line 79). Some critics have decidedly affirmed that the poem is about the inadequacy of the imagination, a rejection of the 'deceiving elf' (line 74). Others see more ambivalence in Keats's attitude. After the possibility of joining the bird in its immortal world has been rejected as a trick of the fancy, they would argue, Keats still suggests through his final question that such vision or transcendent experience is possible, or, at least, still something for which he longs. Is this, ultimately, an escapist poem, or is Keats emphasising the need to accept the human condition, with all the suffering that is associated with it? Compare the ode, in this respect, with the 'Ode on Melancholy'.

**QUESTION**

One of Keats's central preoccupations is the nature and value of dreams. How does he engage with this question in 'Ode to a Nightingale'?

Language is effectively used to create mood. In the opening of the poem, for example, a sense of sluggish weightiness is suggested by the heavy thudding alliterative 'd', 'p', and 'm' when Keats describes his own dull ache. Compare this with the effects created in the second half of the stanza by the light assonantal sounds in such words as 'light' and 'Dryad' (line 7)and the sensuous assonantal sounds of 'beechen', 'green' and 'ease' (lines 9 and 10) when Keats turns to the joy of the nightingale. Compare the vitality and the jubilant tempo of stanza 2 with the dull heaviness and monotony in stanza 3. How are these different effects created? Consider, for a start, the use of repetition, with devices like **parallelism** and **anaphora**. There is a dense concentration of sense impressions in this ode, and a frequent use of **synaesthesia**. In stanza 1, for example, the 'plot' (line 8) where the bird sings is itself 'melodious' and the song contains 'summer' (lines 8 and 10): the visual evokes the aural and the aural the visual. In stanza 2, Keats conveys the taste of wine with reference to colour, action, song and sensation. When Keats says, in stanza 5, 'I cannot see what flowers are at my feet, / Nor what soft incense hangs upon the boughs' (lines 41-2), the suggestion that the incense *could* be seen emphasises the density and headiness of the perfume: it is so strong it seems visible, tangible.

This is often said to be the most personal of the odes. Perhaps it would be better to say that from the abrupt opening of 'My heart aches' onwards, it creates the impression of being the most subjective. Leaving aside the claim by many critics that it is personal in an autobiographical way, how is this impression of subjectivity achieved? It is the processes and movement of the poet's mind that are the central focus of 'Ode to a Nightingale', and the personal 'I' is very much in evidence. In this respect compare the poem with the 'Ode on a Grecian Urn'.

---

**GLOSSARY**

4    **Lethe-wards** (Greek myth) Lethe is one of the rivers of Hades; the dead are obliged to drink from it in order that they may forget everything said and done when alive

7    **Dryad** a tree nymph

16   **Hippocrene** (Greek myth) the fountain of the Muses on Mount Helicon and therefore associated with poetic inspiration; here the term is used to suggest red wine as another source of inspiration

32   **Bacchus and his pards** (Roman myth) the god of wine; the pards are the leopards which draw his chariot

37   **Fays** fairies

51   **Darkling** in the dark

---

## ODE ON A GRECIAN URN 1819 (1820)

**CONTEXT**

The sculptures removed from the Acropolis in Athens by Lord Elgin were purchased for the British Museum two years before this poem was written.

- The poet addresses a Grecian urn.
- He reflects upon its images, which, unlike reality, are eternal.

The poet addresses the urn in stanza 1 as a bride of quietness, a child of time, and a teller of pastoral tales. He asks a series of questions about the scenes depicted upon it. In stanzas 2 and 3 he then describes these scenes in more detail, contrasting the perfection of static art with the imperfection, transience and sorrow of human life. The unheard music depicted on the urn is sweeter than heard music, and unending; since the images are fixed at one moment in time, the lover will always remain at the blissful moment of anticipation; the leaves will never drop from the trees; the object of love will never fade. In stanza 4 he again asks a series of questions, this time concerning a scene of sacrifice. Many people are arriving, and a priest leads a cow to the altar. He speculates about the now empty town from which these people have come. The values represented by the urn are seen from a new and less positive perspective in stanza 5 as the poet, now more detached, reflects upon his own reactions, upon the implications of eternity associated with the urn, and addresses the urn as a 'Cold Pastoral' (line 45). While generations of mortals die, the urn will remain. The ode concludes with the two most perplexing and most debated lines in Keats's poetry, with the urn's assertion that 'Beauty is truth, truth beauty, – that is all / Ye know on earth, and all ye need to know' (lines 49–50).

## COMMENTARY

In this ode, the major contrast is between art and life. The urn, a work of art, seems to represent perfect enduring beauty: human life in contrast is imperfect, transient. The opposition set up, however, does not involve a simple assessment of art as good and life as bad. In the densely metaphorical and paradoxical opening four lines of this ode, the urn is first addressed as a 'still unravish'd bride of quietness' (line 1). Here the word 'still' might suggest 'motionless': the urn is as still, virginal, and perfect as a bride at the altar. On the other hand, the urn is limited: it never changes and the human beings it depicts never experience the fullness and fulfilment of life. Thoughts of eternity cause the poet to reassess the urn and address it as 'Cold Pastoral' (line 45). While the image of the bride may initially appear positive, this second image prompts us to rethink its implications. 'Still' might also mean 'yet': the urn might therefore be seen as sterile and fixed as a bride whose marriage has never been consummated. Perhaps the virtues of durability are outweighed by the disadvantages of fixity.

Consider the descriptions of the scenes depicted on the urn. Do these scenes also simultaneously suggest perfect enduring beauty and cold sterile fixity? There is, for example, the lover. He will

 **CHECK THE BOOK**
An early influential formalist analysis of the verbal and structural effects of 'Ode on a Grecian Urn' can be found in Cleanth Brooks, *The Well Wrought Urn*, Harcourt, 1975.

always be in love with the maiden who will always be fair; he will always be full of the bliss of anticipation. On the other hand, he will never reach the moment of the kiss. Is his love happier than feverish panting human love? The characters depicted may be above all 'breathing human passion' (line 28) that leads to sorrow, but what do they lack as a result? The thought of the emptiness and silence of the deserted town is the deciding factor which turns an eternity of joy and delight into an eternity of desolation. The many paradoxes found in this ode – the urn is silent, for example, but it is also a 'historian' (line 3) that can communicate – effectively suggest the ambivalence that seems to dominate the poem as a whole. If art is the ultimate consolation offered by the ode, art is still nevertheless deathlike: it offers no movement, no change, no fulfilment.

**CHECK THE BOOK**

Donald Keesey's *Contexts for Criticism* (1994) applies three different theoretical approaches to 'Ode on a Grecian Urn'.

The meaning of the last two lines of the ode is perplexing and has been much debated, and these lines may provide, as their aphoristic nature suggests, some kind of summary. But whose summary is it? There is a great deal of uncertainty about where the punctuation should be placed. It could be that the urn speaks both of the final lines; it could be that the urn says only 'Beauty is truth, truth beauty' (line 49) and the remainder should be attributed to the poet. If the latter is the case, then the poet is agreeing with and validating the summary provided by the urn. If the former is the case, as most critics now believe, then we could see him as standing back from what the urn has to offer and say; we do not have to consider this as some kind of clinching summary of the poem's meaning. We also have to consider what the lines 'Beauty is truth, truth beauty' actually mean. This is obviously not truth in a factual sense, as such truths are often not in the least beautiful, but the truth of art, the unflinching representation of all aspects of life. This quality Keats referred to in a letter as 'its intensity'; it is 'capable of making all disagreeable evaporate, from their being in close relationship with Beauty and Truth – Examine King Lear and you will find this exemplified throughout' (*Letters* 1, p. 192). In another letter he wrote: 'What the imagination seizes as Beauty must be truth – whether it existed before or not – for I have the same Idea of all our Passions as of Love they are all in their sublime, creative of essential Beauty' (*Letters* 1, p. 184). Do these comments from Keats throw further light on the meaning of these perplexing last lines? Does he, at this later stage in his life, still believe in these early speculations (see **Themes**, on **Beauty and truth**).

There are significant differences between this ode and the Nightingale ode. Here there is a sense of formality; there is no 'I'; the focus is not so much on a mind at work as on the work of art. As the poem is about a work of art, so the poem also draws attention to the fact that *it* is a work of art. The almost insistent sound patterns, the assonance, the echoes, these and many other stylistic features emphasise the ode's formal status as a poem, its 'literariness'. In the opening two lines, for example, there is the repetition of a long drawn-out 'i' sound; in stanza 2, more repetition in 'unheard echoes heard', 'sweeter sweet', 'pipe pipes' and the specific assonance of 'ear … endear'd', 'spirit ditties', and 'no tone'. There is also the opening series of apostrophes, the frequent use of **parallelism** and **anaphora**, the invocations and exclamations, the constant personifying of the urn. This is emphatically 'poetic' language in that it draws attention to its artifice, to the fact that the poem has been consciously and artfully constructed; there is absolutely no attempt to try to disguise or underplay this artifice and suggest ordinary conversation.

Recent interpretations of this ode have introduced a number of other issues you may wish to consider. In particular they considered the extent to which poetic expression is here also historical expression. What, for example, does the ode represent as masculine or feminine and how are masculinity and femininity defined and characterised? (see **Themes**, on **Women**).

**CHECK THE BOOK**

A discussion of Keats's treatment of Ancient Greek culture can be found in David Ferris's *Silent Urns: Romanticism, Hellenism, Modernity* (2000).

| GLOSSARY | |
|---|---|
| 7 | Tempe  a valley in Thessaly |
| 7 | Arcady  Arcadia, district in Greece, associated with pastoral simplicity and happiness |
| 41 | Attic  from Attica, or Athens |
| 41 | brede  embroidery or decoration |

## ODE ON MELANCHOLY 1819 (1820)

- The poet considers the nature of melancholy.
- He suggests a remedy for this psychological state.
- And he affirms the complex intermingling of the feelings of pleasure and pain, joy and sorrow.

The first stanza begins with a negative imperative insisting that we should not seek escape from the pain of melancholy by resorting to drugs or poisons nor should we make a cult of death. Death would eliminate the awareness, the consciousness, which, though perhaps painful, is still preferable to complete oblivion. It is necessary to maintain the 'wakeful anguish of the soul' (line 10). Instead, the second stanza suggests, a preferable remedy would be to surrender completely to the sensuous aspects of the experience, to feed the melancholy, 'glut' the sorrow (line 15). The third stanza considers the complex and ambiguous nature of melancholy, by presenting a personified Melancholy as a goddess, closely associated with Beauty, Joy and Pleasure, whose shrine is in the temple of Delight. Only those capable of experiencing the most intense joy will know Melancholy. They will, however, also be her victims.

## COMMENTARY

In this ode, which exhorts the reader to seek out beauty and joy no matter what the cost, no matter how much sorrow is associated with them, the central argument is that sensitivity and melancholy are closely linked. To avoid melancholy is to 'drown the wakeful anguish of the soul'( line 10). The correct response is not to avoid it, but to 'glut' (line 15) it. The dominant imagery of the poem is based on the sense of taste, emphasising the need to accept wholeheartedly, to devour, all experience. Melancholy may be linked to sadness and death by the simile in stanza 2 which identifies it as a 'weeping cloud' covering the land with a 'shroud', but melancholy is also nourishing, like the rain which revives the drooping flowers. Keats uses synaesthesia to create rich sensuous impressions in this stanza and to emphasise the need for an acute sensitivity: one must 'glut' one's sorrow on such things as roses. Why is the word 'glut' so much more effective in this context than 'nourish' or 'feed' would be? The need for full involvement is particularly stressed by the complex of sense impressions used in describing the raging mistress. The melancholiac must touch her soft hand, hear her rave, see and taste her peerless eyes. Glut now does give way to 'feed' (line 20), a word which appropriately contributes to the heavy assonance of the line. What effect do these long 'e' sounds have? The imagery of eating continues in stanza 3 with the bee-mouth sipping and eventually culminates in the idea of the grape bursting in the mouth. Melancholy has now become

**QUESTION**

In the 'Ode on Melancholy', does Keats present melancholy as a good thing?

personified as a goddess in the temple of Delight. Her companions are all defined by transience: Beauty must die, Joy is forever leaving, Pleasure constantly turning into poison. Change here is not simply a matter of temporality; in each case, each term contains its opposition within it, a concept most brilliantly captured in the visual image of 'Joy, whose hand is ever at his lips / Bidding adieu' (line 22). The image simultaneously suggests action and stasis, complementing the blended oppositions of joy and sorrow. In this ode Keats no longer even attempts to envision beauty as symbol of some transcendent truth: it is now only one of many elements of a contradictory reality (see **Themes**, on **Beauty and truth**). The person who tastes melancholy to the full lives to the full and this is preferable to oblivion. The taster is also, however, a victim of Melancholy. His soul, now more aware than ever of the transience of happiness, is emptied out, hung up like a battle trophy. This final stanza constantly refers us back to images in the previous two stanzas: the poison of wolf's bane, for example, becomes the Pleasure-poison sipped by the bee-mouth; the ruby grape of Proserpine becomes the grape of Joy; the angry mistress is reflected in the goddess Melancholy.

A gender-oriented reading of this ode might explore exactly why Melancholy is represented as a female figure and why women's anger is presented as one of many spectacles upon which the seeker of pleasure may feed (see **Themes**, on **Women**). A new critical or formalist reading might emphasise the way the poem is structured around the testing and resolution of an argument. The first stanza comprises the thesis: the rejection of oblivion and death. The second stanza offers the antithesis: the assertion of the values of life and experience. The third stanza forms a synthesis: the contradictory ideas of death and life, oblivion and experience are reconciled through paradox. Is this a valid reading? Is there any evidence that contradictions are perhaps not actually reconciled in the end, and that the ode is more open-ended than such a reading suggests?

**CHECK THE BOOK**

John Gerard in his famous *Herball* (1633) describes 'Wolf bane' as 'counted to be very dangerous and deadly...there was never found... Antidote or remedie...this plant is the most poisonous of all others.' Wolf's bane is the popular name for aconite.

**GLOSSARY**

1   **Lethe**  (Greek myth) one of the rivers of Hades; the dead are obliged to drink from it in order that they may forget everything said and done when alive

                                                   continued

> 4  **Proserpine** (Greek myth) Proserpine was captured by Hades and forced to spend six months of each year as queen of the underworld
>
> 7  **Psyche** (Greek) breath, therefore life or the soul itself; also the name of the maiden who loved and lost Cupid and wandered the world in search of her lover

## LAMIA 1819, REVISED 1820 (1820)

- Lamia is transformed from serpent to woman, and lives with Lycius, unseen by the world, in her fairy palace.
- Lycius insists upon marrying her publicly.
- His old tutor comes to the wedding feast, recognises Lamia's true nature and denounces her.
- She disappears and Lycius dies.

**CONTEXT**

In classical mythology, Lamia was a Libyan queen loved by Zeus and robbed of her children by the jealous Hera. She vowed to revenge herself on all children. The race of Lamiae, in Africa, were said to have the head and breast of a woman and the body of a serpent and seduced strangers only to devour them.

In Part 1, the god Hermes, in amorous pursuit of a nymph, encounters Lamia. She has the form of a grotesque serpent, but the mouth and voice of a woman. Lamia promises to restore to him the nymph, whom she has made invisible, if he will in turn restore her to her former human shape. Hermes promises, the nymph appears, and Lamia, after violent convulsions, sheds her skin and a beautiful woman is revealed. She goes to Corinth where she meets and seduces Lycius, the young philosopher of whom she had dreamed and whom she had loved. They retire to a fairy palace which is invisible to everyone in the city, shut away from the 'busy world' (line 397).

Part 2 opens with a blast of trumpets which pierces their secluded magical retreat, prompting Lycius to think of the world outside. Lamia accuses him of wanting to leave her, but he claims that, on the contrary, he simply desires to marry her and make their love known to the world. Lamia, distressed by this idea, pleads with him to change his mind, but eventually submits to his wishes. Lycius arranges a wedding feast to which he invites all his friends. Lamia invites no-one, but, without giving any reasons, begs him not to invite the philosopher Apollonius, his former tutor. Lycius leaves to deliver the invitations and Lamia magically transforms the palace into an elaborate arbour set with a lavish feast. The guests arrive, marvelling at the house they had never noticed before, and Apollonius comes uninvited to the feast. Able to distinguish illusion from reality, Apollonius sees through Lamia's disguise; he fixes his gaze upon the bride and Lycius feels her terror. He denounces Apollonius who replies that he will not see him made a serpent's prey. As he repeats the word 'serpent' and her true nature is disclosed, Lamia vanishes with an awful scream. Lycius, unable to accept the loss of his dream, dies in a frenzy of grief.

## COMMENTARY

With the numerous contrasts it presents – dream and reality, imagination and reason, poetry and philosophy – 'Lamia' has generated more allegorical readings than any other of Keats's poems. The three main characters, Lamia, Lycius and Apollonius, have respectively been read, for example, as poetry, the poet, and the philosopher; as poem, Keats/Poet, and reviewers; and as dream/illusion, the dreamer, reason/reality. Full of shifting perspectives and unresolved tensions, the poem nevertheless ultimately resists all neat diagrammatic links between character and concept. In Keats's source for the events related in this poem, Burton's *Anatomy of Melancholy*, the story is quite straightforward: an innocent young man is rescued from the enchantment of a lamia through the aid of a wise philosopher. In retelling and modifying the story, however, Keats introduced far more ambiguity and complexity, and the poem is coloured by as much ambivalence as the shape-shifting serpent-woman after whom it is named. Keats's most significant modification is the addition of the opening episode concerning Hermes, the nymph and Lamia. What might be the relationship between this introductory episode and the main narrative? Does the former provide an ironic counterpart to the second? We are told that the dreams of gods are real, the implication being that the dreams of mortals are deceptive, unreliable. Mortal lovers are said to grow pale, while immortal lovers do not. The opening episode suggests that in this world of the immortals, love may indeed be simple and easily fulfilled. For Lycius and Lamia in the mortal world, by contrast, love is complex. Although Lamia's dream comes true and she is united with Lycius in a magic palace where an intense and very human passion is reconciled with

**CHECK THE BOOK**

Robert Burton's *The Anatomy of Melancholy* (1621) states that melancholy is 'an inbred malady in everyone of us'. Though a medical book, it is gently **satirical** and packed with interesting and delightful anecdotes.

permanence, this dream of an immortality of passion is no sooner affirmed than it is rejected, shown as an impossibility.

Keats also introduces some ambiguity about where our sympathies should lie. In Part 1, we are alerted to Lamia's real nature, her status as deceptive shape-shifter, her associations with demons and madness. When she foams at the mouth during her transformation, the foam makes the very grass wither and die. There is a clear suggestion that she puts Lycius under a magic spell: when he first meets her and swoons, he is awakened by her kiss 'from one trance … Into another' (Part 1, line 296–7). He is 'tangled in her mesh' (Part 1, line 295), a victim, and she is in complete control. Compare her as she is presented here with the femme fatale of 'La Belle Dame sans Merci' (see **Detailed commentary, Text 3**). In Part 2, however, Lamia loses this control as she in turn becomes the victim of Lycius's human vanity and arrogance. In his overwhelming and pathetic desire to dominate, to parade his 'prize' so that others may be 'confounded and abash'd' (Part 2, lines 57–8), he insists on the public marriage feast. Now he becomes cruel, taking delight in her sorrows, becoming 'fierce and sanguineous' (Part 2, lines 75–6) and he is berated by the narrator as a madman. For the narrator, Lamia's response – 'She burnt, she lov'd the tyranny' (Part 2, line 81) and is subdued – is more than proof of her human nature: 'The serpent – Ha, the serpent! certes, she / Was none' (Part 2, lines 80–1). Lamia has now shape-shifted into a weak woman, with all what the narrator considers to be a mortal woman's predictable qualities. As the lovers alternate between the roles of cruel abuser and innocent victim, our sympathies are split too.

The question is further complicated when we consider the nature of Apollonius. In Burton's original, he is simply the wise sage who saves Lycius. For Keats, who adds the detail of Lycius's death, Apollonius is a sage whose wisdom brings destruction: he is the philosopher who uses reason to save his former pupil, and yet, in the process, kills him. The memorable passage (Part 2, lines 229–38) in which the narrator rhetorically asks 'Do not all charms fly / At the mere touch of cold philosophy' suggests a rejection of pure reason. Does the poem as a whole suggest Keats is completely condemning the 'cold philosophy' which Apollonius embodies and is pleading instead for the primacy of the poetic imagination, the

**QUESTION**

What is the point of prefacing the story of Lamia and Lycius in 'Lamia' with the long account of Hermes and the nymph?

dream world of Lamia? To claim this we have to ignore all her monstrous and deceptive traits as shown in Part 1. In some ways, Apollonius can be seen as performing the same function as the brothers in 'Isabella', bringing the world of cold reality into the lovers' secret and intimate world. And yet Lycius himself is already marked by and a part of this world; it is after all he who wants to expose the 'secret bowers' (Part 2, line 149) of their 'sweet sin' (Part 2, line 31) to 'common eyes' (Part 2, line 149). As a man of Corinth, a city characterised by competition and rivalry, he wants to display Lamia so others can envy his 'prize' (Part 2, line 57).

'Lamia' is written in heroic couplets, lines of iambic pentameter rhymed in pairs. While some of the couplets form closed units, in others the sense is allowed to overrun the couplet rhyme, avoiding the sense of epigrammatic closure. The narrative therefore proceeds briskly, with a continual sense of motion and progression towards one final point. This can be compared with the *ottava rima* of 'Isabella'? where the stanzaic form repeatedly promises and yet withholds closure. There is a similar sense of detachment in the voices of the narrators of the two narratives. Is there cynicism in such asides to the reader as 'Love in a hut, with water and a crust, / Is – Love, forgive us! – cinders, ashes, dust' (Part 2, lines 1–2)?

What other similarities are there between 'Lamia' and the earlier 'Isabella'. To start with, there seems to be a similar intermingling of beauty and horror; does this serve similar functions in the two poems? If you would like to expand your range of comparison to include other Romantic poets, consider Keats's treatment of Lamia in the light of Coleridge's treatment of the serpent woman Geraldine in 'Christabel'.

 **QUESTION**

To what extent can 'Lamia' be read as a repudiation of romantic dreaming?

| GLOSSARY |
|---|
| Part 1 |
| 2-5   Drove ... Fauns   the classical deities of the woodlands were banished by those of medieval folklore, including Oberon, king of the fairies |
| 7   Hermes   messenger of the gods |
| 46   cirque-couchant   in the shape of a circle |
| continued |

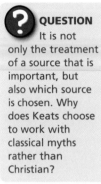

**QUESTION**
It is not only the treatment of a source that is important, but also which source is chosen. Why does Keats choose to work with classical myths rather than Christian?

47    **gordian**   Gordius tied the knot no-one could disentangle; Alexander the Great solved the problem by cutting it with his sword

58    **Ariadne's tiar**   Ariadne's crown, which became a constellation after her death

63    **Proserpine**   carried off by Pluto, Proserpine became queen of Hades

78    **Phœbean dart**   a ray from Phoebus Apollo, god of the sun

81    **star of Lethe**   Hermes led the souls of the dead to Hades

103   **Silenus**   a satyr, tutor of Bacchus, god of wine

133   **Caducean charm**   he touches her with his serpent-entwined staff, the caduceus

163   **rubious-argent**   red and silver

207   **Nereids**   sea nymphs

212   **Mulciber**   another name for Vulcan, god of fire and metal-working

248   **Orpheus-like … Eurydice**   Orpheus was allowed to lead his wife Eurydice back from Hades on the condition he did not look back at her. He did, and lost her for ever

265   **Pleiad**   one of the seven Pleiades, daughters of Atlas, who were transformed into stars

320   **Adonian feast**   feast of Adonis, who was beloved by Venus

329   **Peris**   in Persian mythology, fairy-like beings

333   **Pyrrha's pebbles**   Pyrrha and Deucalian repeopled the earth after the flood by scattering stones which turned into human beings

386   **Aeolian**   like sounds from an Aeolian harp, an instrument which plays when the wind blows through it; the name comes from Aeolus, god of the winds

**Part 2**

160   **daft**   puzzled

185   **libbard's**   leopard's

187   **Ceres' horn**   the horn of plenty

226   **thyrsus**   the vine-entwined staff of Bacchus, god of wine

264   **myrtle**   sacred to Venus, goddess of love

## THE FALL OF HYPERION 1819 (1857)

- The poet-speaker dreams of meeting Moneta.
- She allows him to witness through her revealed memories the fall of the Titans.

Canto 1 begins with the poet-speaker's declaration that everyone has the capacity to dream. The dreams of the poet, however, are superior to the dreams of fanatics and savages. He then describes how he found himself, in a dream, within a luxuriant forest full of exotic trees, fragrant blossoms and the gentle showers of fountains. Here, before an empty arbour, he discovers the remnants of a feast of summer fruits. He eats these and pledges 'all the mortals of the world' with a glass of 'transparent juice' (Canto 1, lines 42–4). This contains the drug that launches him into another world. He falls into a swoon, awakening to find himself in a far sterner landscape where there is an abandoned temple. Approaching the altar, he sees a staircase. A voice warns 'If thou canst not ascend / These steps, die on that marble where thou art' (Canto 1, lines 108–9). In spite of the icy cold which threatens to destroy him, he manages to gain the steps and is restored by their life-giving powers. At the top, he encounters a veiled Shadow, the keeper of an ancient flame. He is told he has been saved because those who climb are aware of the world's miseries and concerned to change them. The shadow nevertheless considers him a dreaming thing aspiring to visionary experience. He responds that not all poets are ineffectual, that a poet is a sage, a humanist and physician to all men, although he doubts that he himself actually fills this role. The shadow tells him that the true poet and the dreamer are distinct and that he is only of the dreamer-tribe. This he rejects, however, attacking such false poets. The Shadow then reveals herself as Moneta, a counterpart of Mnemosyne from *Hyperion*, and unveils herself, revealing a face of unearthly pallor and immortal suffering. The poet longs to see what high tragedy is being acted out within the 'dark secret Chambers of her skull' (Canto 1, line 278). Moneta agrees to reveal to him her memories of the fall of the Titans and at this point Keats picks up the story of the defeated Saturn from the first *Hyperion*.

> **CONTEXT**
>
> Keats had given up trying to finish *Hyperion* in 1818. The following year he began rewriting and recasting it as 'The Fall of Hyperion'. But he would once more give up the attempt to complete it.

Canto 2, which is unfinished, opens with Moneta's description of the palace of Hyperion. Moneta and the poet witness the arrival of the sun-god and the narrative breaks off.

## COMMENTARY

The central concern of 'The Fall of Hyperion' is the nature of the true poet. The ability to dream Keats now considers universal, the visionary capacity shared by 'every man whose soul is not a clod' (Canto 1, line 13). The poet achieves greatness not because of any special insight but because of his gift of language and his ability to share the world's sorrows, to participate imaginatively in all human existence and comfort man in his anguish. The poet-speaker's progress within the poem is towards this necessary full awareness of human suffering. In this context, consider why are we given two different dreams: one in a lush forest and one in a bleak and austere landscape. By participating in Moneta's grief the narrator becomes both a fellow sufferer and a poet to whom the sorrows of the Titans foreshadow the miseries of the world. Compare the notion of progression found here, as well as the movement from garden of delight to imposing temple, with Keats's parable of life as a 'Mansion of Many Apartments' as outlined in the letter to John Hamilton Reynolds of 3 May 1818 (*Letters* 1, pp. 280–1) (see **Themes**).

One factor that complicates any reading of the poem is the uncertain and sometimes contradictory attitude towards dreams. Keats's new version of the story of Hyperion is cast in the form of a dream vision, a literary device that dates back to such medieval writers as Chaucer and Dante. Paradoxically, however, within this dream vision there is an attack on dreams. As Moneta says in some of Keats's most famous lines:

> The poet and the dreamer are distinct
> Diverse, sheer opposites, antipodes.
> The one pours out a balm upon the world,
> The other vexes it
>
> (Canto 1, lines 199–202)

Look specifically at the initial dialogue between Keats and Moneta and consider the various attempts to define the poet and distinguish him from the dreamer. Are these attempts ultimately successful or repeatedly frustrated? Does the paradox that an attack on dreamers takes places within a dream help to clarify exactly what Keats is claiming to be the function of the true poet? Does the poem ever fully clarify the difference between the dreams of the poet and the dreams of the fanatic or savage described in the Induction?

**QUESTION**
How are attempts to define the poet and distinguish him from the dreamer frustrated at the same time as they are articulated?

Moneta, the Latin counterpart of the Greek Mnemosyne in *Hyperion*, is goddess of Memory. She is one of the fallen Titans, now sole priestess of Saturn's desolation. For the poet, she functions as a Dantean guide: as Virgil and Beatrice guide Dante through hell, purgatory, and heaven, so she guides this poet through a kind of classical purgatory where the deposed Titans mourn the loss of empire. Moneta has been called the most powerful female figure in Keats's poetry, and also the most articulate (see **Themes**, on **Women**). It has also been suggested that the poet-speaker here is Keats's weakest male; what evidence is there for this? Moneta can also be seen as maternal, and the mother figure is often considered the most powerful feminine figure in Romantic poetry generally. In complete contrast to the sexually desirable female immortals of many earlier poems, Moneta is the mother with 'minist'ring' power (Canto 1, line 96) who is the agent of rebirth and self-knowledge, rather than the sexually threatening lover who must be controlled. What other characteristics can be ascribed to Moneta: is she admonitory and judgemental, consoling and inspiring or perhaps all these? Moneta is in some ways also the ideal poet: she is able to contain and endure suffering and still teach others its lessons. This is most notably suggested in the impressive lines which describe her face (Canto 1, lines 256–71), lines which encapsulate one of the essential beliefs of the later Keats: the necessity and beauty of suffering.

*Hyperion*, influenced by Milton, is structured as an epic with a detached narrator of an heroic story. In 'The Fall of Hyperion' epic objectivity is replaced by intense lyricism, epic fable by personal myth. There are far fewer epithets, epic similes, and catalogues in this reworking of the myth. The later poem is generally less crowded with imagery, less concerned with the patterning of lines, and the language is more colloquial, more relaxed. Elements specifically inspired by *Paradise Lost*, including the debate of the fallen Titans which echoes the fallen angels in hell, are abandoned. This moves the focus to suffering, eliminating hope that remained in the earlier version. Even Saturn's defiance is downplayed, and his

**?** **QUESTION**
Keats left off writing 'The Fall of Hyperion' at the moment he started 'To Autumn'. What is the difference in the ways the two poems deal with change?

speech full of words like 'feebleness' and (repeated twelve times) 'moan'. What is the effect of the descriptions of the fallen Titans being presented by the sorrowing Moneta rather than the detached epic narrator of *Hyperion*? 'The Fall of Hyperion' is more influenced by Dante than Milton, in such matters as the use of the dream vision and the guide and the replacement of Miltonic books with Dantean cantos. While in *Hyperion*, Keats is interested in change, here he is interested in the effects of change, with the way in which beauty and sorrow coexist, with the nature of the poet; the fall of the Titans is consequently no longer the focus of the poem.

As a means of identifying some specific examples of the differences suggested above, compare the ways in which Hyperion himself is represented in the two poems. Alternatively, examine the corresponding sections which describe the arrival of Thea, her exchanges with Saturn and their departure to meet their fellow Titans. (*Hyperion*, 1, lines 22–157; 'The Fall of Hyperion. A Dream', 1, lines 327–468). Many of the lines are the same, but the meaning and tone of the two passages are quite different. Such a comparison also demonstrates more generally how Keats's style has developed and could suggest the direction his work might have taken if he had lived longer.

| GLOSSARY |
|---|
| Canto 1 |
| 35  fabled horn  the horn of plenty |
| 37  Proserpine  queen of Hades who had to spend six months of each year in the underworld; her return to earth each year marks the coming of spring |
| 48  Caliphat  government of Muslim world |
| 50  scarlet **conclave** college of Cardinals |
| 56  Silenus  satyr and tutor of Bacchus, god of wine |
| 96  One minist'ring  the Roman Moneta, goddess of memory, who now substitutes for the Greek Mnemosyne in the first Hyperion |
| 103  maian  Maia was one of the Pleiades, the daughters of Atlas transformed into stars |
| 203  Pythia  priestess of the oracle of Apollo at Delphi |
| 288  Omega  final letter of the Greek alphabet |
| 312  zoning  course |

## EXTENDED COMMENTARIES

# TEXT 1 - TO AUTUMN

**1**

Season of mists and mellow fruitfulness,
Close bosom-friend of the maturing sun;
Conspiring with him how to load and bless
With fruit the vines that round the thatch-eves run;
To bend with apples the moss'd cottage-trees,
And fill all fruit with ripeness to the core;
To swell the gourd, and plump the hazel shells
With a sweet kernel; to set budding more,
And still more, later flowers for the bees,
Until they think warm days will never cease,
For Summer has o'er-brimm'd their clammy cells.

**2**

Who hath not seen thee oft amid thy store?
Sometimes whoever seeks abroad may find
Thee sitting careless on a granary floor,
Thy hair soft-lifted by the winnowing wind;
Or on a half-reaped furrow sound asleep,
Drows'd with the fume of poppies, while thy hook
Spares the next swath and all its twined flowers:
And sometimes like a gleaner thou dost keep
Steady thy laden head across a brook;
Or by a cyder-press, with patient look,
Thou watchest the last oozings hours by hours.

**3**

Where are the songs of Spring? Ay, where are they?
Think not of them, thou hast thy music too, -
While barred clouds bloom the soft-dying day,
And touch the stubble-plains with rosy hue;
Then in a wailful choir the small gnats mourn
Among the river sallows, borne aloft
Or sinking as the light wind lives or dies;
And full-grown lambs loud bleat from hilly bourn;
Hedge-crickets sing; and now with treble soft
The red-breast whistles from a garden-croft;
And gathering swallows twitter in the skies.

 **CHECK THE NET**

Images of the cornfield: of sowing, harvesting, gleaning, winnowing, all became very popular themes for nineteenth-century painters, such as Jean-François Millet (1814–75) and Samuel Palmer (1805–81). Check them on the net.

**CHECK THE NET**

To hear a selection of readers recite 'To Autumn' see http://www. theatlantic.com/ unbound/poetry/ soundings/keats. htm. The site includes a discussion of the poem.

While 'To Autumn' has not, overall, attracted the same amount of critical attention as the other odes, it was particularly admired by the formalists who dominated critical thought until the mid twentieth century, and frequently described as the most 'perfect' and 'flawless' of Keats's poems. The following analysis of 'To Autumn' will offer such a formalist approach, excluding what is external to the poem, such as social, political, or biographical considerations, and emphasising matters of form and style to demonstrate the 'literariness' of the text. Close reading can still be a useful way to begin an exploration of a text.

This valedictory poem, this consolatory farewell to the season, has been particularly praised for its controlled symmetry and balance. A good place to begin, then, is with its formal structure. Symmetry and balance are evident in various aspects of the stanzaic progression; try to find specific evidence to back up the general movements that will be described. There is a seasonal movement from early autumn (1) to high autumn (2) to late autumn (3), and a corresponding movement from ripening to harvesting and storing to the barrenness of 'stubble-plains' (line 26). There is even a movement in the dominant form of imagery in each stanza from the tactile (1), to the visual (2), to the auditory (3). Why does the poem progressively emphasise these particular senses? Helen Vendler has also noted symmetry in the parallelism of syntactical units in each stanza. In the first stanza, the dominant syntactical unit is the infinitive ('to load', 'to bend'). What are the dominant syntactical forms of the other stanzas? Balance is also achieved by the way the first and third stanzas focus on descriptions of the landscape, on the work of nature, while the middle stanza, by focusing on the humanised figure of Autumn, brings in the work of men and women.

To continue with the idea of balance, consider the various ways in which Keats combines images of process and stasis. Could we claim, with the New Critics, that these tensions, oppositions, are ultimately reconciled, creating unity within the text? The opening stanza conveys this feeling of stasis through images of fulfilment, maturity, ripeness. At the same time, however, Keats draws upon verbs suggestive of continuing activity; the sun conspires with autumn to 'set budding more, / And still more, later flowers for the bees, / Until they think warm days will never cease' (lines 9–10). If here there is movement and process in the midst of stillness and fulfilment, in the next stanza there is stillness where we expect movement. Autumn is now imagined as various figures with the harvest scene. Where we would expect action in the harvesting and gleaning, the main mood is one of lethargic blissfulness, a sense of repletion and serenity. Autumn sits on the granary floor or sleeps; movement is momentarily suggested by the image of Autumn the gleaner crossing a brook, and then we return to stillness as Autumn patiently watches, 'hours by hours' (line 22), the pressing of the apples into cider. Does this conflation of stasis and process continue in the third stanza? In this ode Keats uses an eleven-line stanza, one more line per stanza than the other odes. What is the effect of the addition of this extra line? Particularly since it is preceded by a couplet, with all its associations of closure, the extra line could be said to establish formally the notion of overflowing abundance described by the poet. All the features of the structure that have been discussed emphasise conscious design or patterning and the 'literariness' of the ode.

Although questions of language have already been briefly touched upon in this discussion of structure, let us now turn to examine the 'literariness' of the language in more detail. Its most striking characteristic is its highly pictorial and sensuous nature; even the most abstract of thoughts is conveyed in a concrete form. You should also be able to find examples of various specific types of images and rhetorical devices in this ode, but the dominant image is clearly personification. The ode begins with an apostrophe to a personified Autumn, 'bosom friend' of the 'maturing sun', and, through a list enumerating the various maturing fruits and flowers, conveys a sense of overflowing ripeness and plenitude. This sense of heavy abundance is further conveyed in such syntactic doublings as 'mists and mellow fruitfulness', in the multiple nouns and verbs, and in the numerous long vowel sounds and clusters of consonants that force one to read slowly. That weightiness and abundance, however, are combined with a sense of vitality in the active verbs: vine are *loaded* with fruit, trees are *bent* with the weight of apples. Are there other examples? How does the language change in the second stanza? Does the language begin to enact the movement from an emphasis on process to an emphasis on stasis? What are the effects of the subtle pattern of alliteration and assonantal sounds? The

 **QUESTION**

What is the relationship between the actual and the ideal in 'Ode to Autumn'?

 **CHECK THE BOOK**

On the politics of 'To Autumn', see Andrew Bennet, *Keats, Narrative and Audience: The Posthumous Life of Writing*, pp. 159–71.

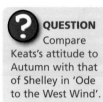

**QUESTION**
Compare Keats's attitude to Autumn with that of Shelley in 'Ode to the West Wind'.

suggestion of a movement towards conclusion, towards death, in the last – and consider the striking effect of this colloquial word – 'oozings' of the second stanza is taken up in the final stanza. 'Where are the songs of Spring?' (line 23) he – or is it Autumn – asks, effectively combining synecdoche and personification. Rejecting these, he instead enumerates the music of Autumn. Now he moves towards images suggestive of death: the 'soft-dying day' (line 25)and the small gnats who 'mourn'(line 27). These images, however, are followed by descriptions of singing crickets and twittering swallows. Such simple and lively onomatopoeic words as 'whistles' and 'twitter' (lines 32 and 33) function to offset the weightiness of death with a sense of the vitality of life. The poem ends, therefore, as it begins: stasis and process are still joined.

In following formalist methodologies, this analysis has been concerned with the 'literariness' of the poem, on form, style, technique, and an emphasis has been placed on unity, balance, symmetry. Many critics would no doubt find evidence that this supposed unity is actually compromised in the poem; is it possible to question the reconciliation of oppositions that has been implied?

With the exception of one reference to the other odes, the poem has been treated as an autonomous whole. Critics have identified, however, a wealth of intertextual references, ranging from Virgil to Shakespeare to Wordsworth. Would it enrich an understanding of the poem to recall, for example, Shakespeare's autumnal trees with their bare ruined choirs in the sonnet 'That time of year thou mayst in me behold'?

Little attempt has been made to suggest what the poem might 'mean'. You may find it useful to read the ode with reference to some of the ideas discussed in the **Critical approaches** section. What, for example, is the relationship in this poem between the actual and the ideal? Does Keats still long for some transcendent vision? Where does he seem to locate what is of value in the ode? How does this relate to his views on mutability and permanence?

Finally, this analysis of 'To Autumn' has made no reference to anything external to the poem. The decade in which it was written, however, was one of severe economic and political crisis. There were widespread food riots, demands for electoral reform, work opportunities, better wages and lower prices. The Peterloo Massacre occurred one month before Keats composed this poem. Would a knowledge of these events change your reading of the poem? Historicist critics have generally considered 'To Autumn' as an attempt to evade or repress the disruptions of history. An intriguing discussion which demonstrates how it is actually a *strategic* suppression of history, an effacement of the oppressed, may be found in Andrew Bennett's *Keats, Narrative, and Audience* (Cambridge University Press, 1994). Consider the gleaner. In this age of industrial development and agrarian unrest, what might have been the actual situation of that gleaner; would he have been benefiting from the luxurious abundances of Keats's Autumn? Who or what is being silenced here?

**CONTEXT**

On the day of the 'Peterloo Massacre' of August 1819, 60,000 people gathered in St Peter's Fields, Manchester, in support of parliamentary reform; the local magistrates, after allowing the meeting, decided to arrest the speakers, and sent in first the constabulary, then the Yeomanry, and finally the Fifteenth Hussars, professional soldiers who were wearing the battle colours they had worn at Waterloo; the crowd was violently dispersed, eleven killed and many hundreds injured.

## TEXT 2 – ON FIRST LOOKING INTO CHAPMAN'S HOMER

Much have I travell'd in the realms of gold,
 And many goodly states and kingdoms seen;
 Round many western islands have I been
Which bards in fealty to Apollo hold.
Oft of one wide expanse had I been told
 That deep-brow'd Homer ruled as his demesne;
 Yet did I never breathe its pure serene
Till I heard Chapman speak out loud and bold:
Then felt I like some watcher of the skies
 When a new planet swims into his ken;
Or like stout Cortez when with eagle eyes
 He star'd at the Pacific – and all his men
Look'd at each other with a wild surmise –
 Silent, upon a peak in Darien.

'On first looking into Chapman's Homer', written in 1816 after Keats came across the translation by George Chapman of *The Whole Works of Homer* (1614), is generally considered to be his first major poem. Keats here makes particularly effective use of the natural divisions of the **Petrarchan sonnet**. The theme of exploration dominates the **octave**, with the **metaphor** of the poet as literary adventurer, and this is followed by the theme of discovery

**CONTEXT**

By the time Keats came to read Homer, a number of translations existed. As well as Chapman's version, Alexander Pope (1688–1740) had produced versions of both the *Iliad* and the *Odyssey* in the 1720s, which, though much admired throughout the eighteenth and nineteenth centuries, did not faithfully reflect either the spirit or diction of the originals.

in the sestet, with the use of similes through which Keats attempts to convey his wonder. The pivotal moment of the sonnet, the volta which prompts the turn from one theme to the other, is the reading of Chapman's Homer. This sonnet has been much admired for its power and directness, particularly the last four lines, with the sense of awe so strikingly conveyed by the image of Cortez on a mountain peak, staring at the Pacific while his men wait, wondering what overwhelming sight has produced this state of frozen amazement and exaltation in their leader. What is the effect of the patterns of alliteration in the final lines and how does this influence the pace of reading? A powerful contrast is made between calm stillness and agitated movement. All the energy and action associated with exploration and all the excitement suggested by the 'wild surmise' (line 13) of the men give way to the awe and silence produced at the moment of discovery. Awe is emphasised by the effective foregrounding of the word 'Silent' in the last line; emphasis is thrown upon the word by the way we are forced to wait, while Keats describes the men, for the description of their leader to be completed. While their historical discovery produces silence, Keats's poetical discovery produces a poem.

Keats actually confuses Cortez (1485–1547), who conquered Mexico, with Balboa (1475–1519) who was the first explorer to see the Pacific. Nevertheless, the historical specificity of the image contributes greatly to the success of the poem. Would the lines have been as compelling if he had used general terms like 'explorer', 'ocean', and 'mountain' instead of 'Cortez', 'Pacific', and 'Darien'?

This is one of the many poems on which historicist critics have focused over the last twenty years in challenging the idea of a dehistoricised and depoliticised Keats (see Critical History). The challenge has come from both traditional, historically based literary criticism, which contextualises the work with reference to the events and ideas of the age, and the new historicism, which focuses more on the production, transmission and reception of the text in literary history. After briefly contextualising the sonnet with respect to Keats's sources, the following analysis will deal primarily with the latter.

Keats's source for information about the 'discovery' of the new world, William Robertson's *History of America*, provides a strangely contradictory account of the Spanish explorers. On the one hand Robertson offers a highly romanticised account which focuses on the strange and marvellous discoveries they made and their admiring wonder. On the other hand Robertson strongly qualifies their achievements by arguing that their missions were prompted by greed, personal ambition and a particularly brutal form of imperialism, involving the large-scale abuse and slaughter of the native populations.

Keats's sonnet can be said to present exploration and colonisation as the work of the poet. As he moves from his own discovery of Chapman's classical literary world to the Spanish explorers' discovery of the New World, historical and imaginative processes are linked by a common concern with territory and conquest. By linking his own discovery to that of the explorers, he affirms the poet's imaginative ability to disclose the wonders of the world. As Keats appropriates these historical discoveries for his sonnet of imaginative discovery, does the poem ignore the grim political realities to which Robertson refers, the pillaging and spoliation? It has been suggested that while the opening address to the 'realms of gold' refers to the traditions of poetry with which Keats was so familiar, it simultaneously draws our attention to the underlying motives of New World exploration. As the critics have demonstrated, Keats frequently uses images of gold to suggest the greed or cultural impoverishment of nineteenth-century capitalist society. We see this, for example, in the outburst against the brothers in 'Isabella' and in the description of Lamia's palace. Leaving aside the vexed question of whether Keats *intended* the gold reference here to have any negative connotations, could the reference point to ways in which his literary imperialism enacts the desire for personal gain or glory demonstrated in historical imperialism?

In Robertson, Balboa's search for the Pacific Ocean is motivated by a desire to rival and even exceed the discoveries of his predecessor Columbus; his, then, is certainly a personal quest for glory. Marjorie Levinson, who associates Keats's relation to literary tradition with nineteenth-century class struggles, suggests that as the explorers pillaged the New World, so Keats pillages, by means of Chapman's translation, Homer and Greek culture. What are his motives? With

> **? QUESTION**
>
> For some critics, the speaking 'I' in Keats's poetry is represented in the traditionally feminine pose of passivity. Is this a valid assessment of the 'I' who speaks in his odes? What about his sonnets?

the growth of commerce and trade, the social classes of this new industrial world were being renegotiated, and Keats was in an unstable social position. He has been variously described as being of lower-class or lower-middle-class origins. The confusion gives credence to Andrew Motion's suggestion that Keats himself was unsure if he was climbing out of the former or slipping out of the latter (*Keats*, 1997, p. xxiv). Keats was certainly full of anxieties about his social background and about his education, and this sonnet was included in his first published volume, when he was still unsure about himself as a poet. Perhaps, then, Keats's literary explorations do reflect a desire for personal enhancement of some kind. Perhaps the sonnet reveals Keats's attempt to claim for himself a place within the main literary tradition, to authorise and legitimise a sense of himself as a poet.

Vincent Newey argues that Keats's awareness of his status as an 'outsider' is evident within the sonnet. 'Round many western islands have I been' (line 3), Keats tells us. This 'intending poet', Newey argues, only 'circumnavigates the place' established poets occupy. He is presently on the periphery, but he wants to be within the hallowed circle and has staked his claim to this territory. 'He seeks to empower himself, by right, *within* a culture which, though available, is his neither by birth nor even upbringing' ('Keats, history, and the poets' in *Keats and History*, ed. N. Roe, pp. 183–4). Moving away from a strictly literary reading to a wider socio-economic reading, does the desire for advancement revealed in the sonnet enact the desires of the aspiring classes in the capitalist, imperialist society of the time?

If Keats was revealing his aspirations and authorising his poetic ambitions, it is particularly interesting to note the kind of attention the sonnet attracted in John Gibson Lockhart's abusive review of *Endymion* and *Poems* (1817) in *Blackwood's Magazine*, Keats, Lockhart sneered, knew Homer only through Chapman. What Lockhart implies is that not only is this young *parvenu* incapable of reading Homer in the original Greek, but that the translation he chooses is Chapman's eccentric Elizabethan version, and not the more elegant eighteenth-century production of Pope, which was, at the time, far more admired. Keats is, then, dismissively defined as an outsider and an upstart. In his very attempt to claim for himself a

**CONTEXT**

Keats's father had been an ostler, that is, he ran a stable at an inn, where travellers could hire horses for their next part of the journey.

place within literary tradition he provides the literary establishment with the ammunition to exclude him further.

## TEXT 3 – LA BELLE DAME SANS MERCI

1
O what can ail thee, knight-at-arms,
  Alone and palely loitering?
The sedge has wither'd from the lake,
  And no birds sing.

II
O what can ail thee, knight-at-arms,
  So haggard and so woe-begone?
The squirrel's granary is full,
  And the harvest's done.

III
I see a lilly on thy brow,
  With anguish moist and fever dew,
And on thy cheeks a fading rose
  Fast withereth too.

IV
I met a lady in the meads,
  Full beautiful – a faery's child,
Her hair was long, her foot was light,
  And her eyes were wild.

V
I made a garland for her head,
  And bracelets too, and fragrant zone;
She look'd at me as she did love,
  And made sweet moan.

VI
I set her on my pacing steed,
  And nothing else saw all day long,
For sidelong would she bend, and sing
  A faery's song.

**QUESTION**
How does the landscape reflect the situation of the knight-at-arms?

**QUESTION**
Does the Knight answer the question he is asked?

VII

She found me roots of relish sweet,
  And honey wild, and manna dew,
And sure in language strange she said –
  'I love thee true'.

VIII

She took me to her elfin grot,
  And there she wept, and sigh'd full sore,
And there I shut her wild wild eyes
  With kisses four.

IX

And there she lulled me asleep,
  And there I dream'd – Ah! woe betide!
The latest dream I ever dream'd
  On the cold hill side.

X

I saw pale kings and princes too,
  Pale warriors, death-pale were they all;
They cried – 'La Belle Dame sans Merci
  Hath thee in thrall!'

XI

I saw their starved lips in the gloam,
  With horrid warning gaped wide,
And I awoke and found me here,
  On the cold hill's side.

XII

And this is why I sojourn here,
  Alone and palely loitering,
Though the sedge has wither'd from the lake,
  And no birds sing.

'La Belle Dame sans Merci' or 'The Beautiful Lady without Pity' is the title of an early fifteenth-century French poem by Alain Chartier which belongs to the tradition of courtly love. Keats appropriates this phrase for a ballad which has been generally read as the story of a seductive and treacherous woman who tempts men away from the real world and then leaves them, their dreams unfulfilled and their lives blighted. For all the beguiling simplicity of the surfaces of this literary ballad, it is one of the most difficult of Keats's poems to explain, and open to many interpretations. It has been alternately suggested, for example, that it is about the wasting power of sexual love and/or the poet's infatuation with his muse. This particular analysis will examine the 'La Belle Dame sans Merci' as a poem about a *femme fatale* and offer a **feminist** interpretation of the ballad. A *femme fatale* or fatal woman conventionally tempts man with her beauty and ultimately causes his destruction. There are many such figures in traditional supernatural ballads concerned with a faery's seduction of a human; notable examples include Tam Lin and Thomas the Rhymer.

That the knight-at-arms in this poem has been enchanted, enthralled, is immediately suggested by his wandering in a desolate wasteland where the plant life has withered and no birds sing. He himself is in a decline; he is pale and the rose in his cheeks, like the sedge, is withering. In trying to explain his state to his questioner, he makes us highly suspicious of the lady whom he encountered. What is there in his description that makes the lady sound dangerous? To start with, he identifies her as a supernatural being, a 'faery's child' with 'wild wild eyes' (lines 14 and 31) suggestive perhaps of madness. She speaks a strange language, and in her elfin grotto she lulls him to sleep. There may be a suggestion here that she is potentially treacherous since 'lulled' (line 33) can denote an attempt to calm someone's fears or suspicions by deception. The lady's responsibility for his condition seems to be confirmed in the dream he has of the death of pale kings, princes, and warriors who claim 'La Belle Dame sans Merci / Hath thee in thrall!' (lines 39-40). 'And this is why I sojourn here' (line 45), he tells his questioner, apparently referring back to this 'horrid warning' of the dream. He stays because he is in thrall to the beautiful lady without pity.

A haunting ominous effect is created through Keats's use of the formal features of the traditional ballad. Frequent repetition is one such feature; in the original oral ballad form this would have been an aid to memory as well as emphasising particular points when the poem was recited. What is the effect of repetitions of words,

**CHECK THE BOOK**

An analysis of visual representations of 'La Belle Dame sans Merci' can be found in Grant Scott's article, 'Language Strange: A Visual History of Keats's "La Belle Dame sans Merci', in *Studies in Romanticism*, 38.4 (1999), pp. 503–35.

**CHECK THE NET**

Compare Keats's 'La Belle Dame' with the traditional ballad, Thomas Rhymer. See text at http://skell.org/SKELL/rhymer.htm.

phrases, and lines in Keats's literary ballad? Repetition is also found in the alliterative and assonantal effects of such lines as 'Her hair was long, her foot was light', 'made sweet moan' (lines 15, 20), and 'wild wild eyes' (line 31). Also following the ballad manner, the words are deployed tersely. Why might Keats choose such language in striking contrast to his more usual luxuriant mode? Although he follows tradition in using a four-line stanza or quatrain rhyming *abcb*, he makes one notable adjustment. Normally a ballad line has about eight syllables with four stresses in the first and third lines and three in the second and fourth. Keats shortens the last line of each stanza: it has only two stresses and usually only four syllables. This creates the effect of the stanza being abruptly cut off, of something being absent or withheld. So exactly what is being withheld in this poem?

We are, in fact, given very little information about anything. We know nothing about the speaker who interrogates and describes the knight. We know very little about the lady, only what the knight tells us; we are offered no interpretation of his experience; indeed, the knight's story opens up more questions than it answers. What is the significance of this lady and why should she want to enthral the knight? Let us turn back to the 'belle dame' then, but, rather than focusing on what he tells us she does to him, let us consider what he says he does to her. The knight is hardly just a helpless victim. He courts her, and creates garlands and bracelets and belts that can be seen not only to decorate but also to bind and enclose her. He claims possession of her: 'I set her on my pacing steed' (line 21). As soon as they reach her 'elfin grot' (line 29), we are given the perplexing and unexplained suggestion that she herself is now unhappy: 'she wept, and sigh'd full sore' (line 30). The lady has been defined as a cruel enchantress, but does she actually do anything that can be said to be cruel or enthralling? Does she even seduce him? If she speaks in 'language strange' (line 27), how can he be sure she said 'I love thee true' (line 27). It would seem that he translates what she says into what he wants to hear. Once we question his translation of her words we are also forced back to question the lines 'She look'd at me as she did love, / And made sweet moan' (lines 19-20). How do we read the ambiguous syntax here: does he mean she looked at him while she loved him or she looked at him as though she did love him?

A feminist critic might point to the many ambiguities, contradictions and lacunae in the text to offer a counterreading in which it is the lady who is, in a sense, the victim. Such a reading would focus less on her actual identity, which we can know little about anyway, and more on the patriarchal order which defines and interprets her identity. See feminism in **Literary terms** for a list of patriarchally defined male/female attributes. Are there any binary oppositions established in the poem which might fit with this set of oppositions?

Who defines the lady as 'la belle dame sans merci', as the *femme fatale* in this ballad? Keats places the definers and interpreters firmly within the patriarchal world. It is the knight who tells the story, who describes the lady for us and his questioner. The knight and the kings, princes and warriors who appear in his dream, belong to the masculine world of strife and action, government and politics. All have been attracted to the feminine bower world of the lady and her 'elfin grot'; they have luxuriated in the pleasures she has provided. They have succumbed not so much to the lady but to something within themselves which desires to withdraw from the masculine world of duties and responsibilities. The lady provides the knight with sweet foods and lulls him to sleep. Now we are trying to see things from her perspective, we become more aware of the extremely ambiguous nature of that word 'lulled'. It can indeed mean to calm someone's fears or suspicions by deception. It can also, however, more innocently mean to soothe with soft sounds and motions, as a mother might soothe a child to sleep. We can assume that the pale kings and warriors with 'starved lips' (line 41) have had a similar experiences to the knight. In the lady's world they regress in an almost infantile manner. Then, recognising that the power and stability of the patriarchal world depends on the rejection of this urge to withdraw, the kings, warriors, and princes have placed the blame squarely upon the woman, defined her as the temptress who has the knight in thrall. And the knight seems to authorise this definition: 'And this is why I sojourn here' (line 45), he tells his questioner. Wandering in this barren landscape, he is neither in the masculine world of strife and action nor the feminine world of the bower. In succumbing to his desire to withdraw from the duties and responsibilities of the former into the luxurious pleasures of the latter he has undermined the definitions and

**QUESTION**

Compare the ways in which the serpent women in 'Lamia' and the belle dame in 'La Belle Dame sans Merci' are set in opposition to the worlds of adult responsibility. Does Keats come to the same conclusions with respect to the ensuing conflict in the two poems?

**QUESTION**

Discuss the ways in which Keats uses the natural world to comment upon human relationships in two or three poems of your choice.

assigned roles of male and female. Now neither is open to him; he is in limbo. A reading such as given above would fit well with Keats's general ambivalence concerning romance and the bower. Would it further illuminate such figures as the serpent woman 'Lamia' and the 'Fair plumed Syren' 'Romance' in 'On sitting down to read King Lear once again'?

# PART THREE

# CRITICAL APPROACHES

## THEMES

### POETRY AND THE POET

Many of Keats's major poems deal specifically with the nature of poetry and the poet. A number of the key concepts in Keats's poetic thought are outlined in the following discussion of themes; these concepts will be discussed with reference to both the letters and the poems.

### PERMANENCE AND MUTABILITY

Before he turned fifteen Keats had lost his parents, an infant brother, an uncle and his grandfather. His apprenticeship with a surgeon and his training at Guy's Hospital exposed him to every kind of human suffering. He nursed his brother Tom until he died of tuberculosis, and was well aware of the implications of its symptoms that he himself experienced in the following four years which preceded his early death. Given the frequent reminders of mortality in his own life, it is hardly surprising that as a poet Keats should be acutely concerned with mutability. He had first-hand knowledge of what he describes in 'Ode to a Nightingale' as the 'weariness, the fever, and the fret' (line 23) of the human condition, of the world where 'men sit and hear each other groan' (line 24) and 'youth grows pale, and spectre-thin, and dies' (line 26), a world where nothing remains constant, and even 'Beauty cannot keep her lustrous eyes, / Or new Love pine at them beyond to-morrow' (lines 23–30). Many of the poems reveal his attempt through the visionary imagination to identify something which is essential and permanent, but for the mature Keats this quest is always tempered by his ultimate **paradoxical** recognition that what is of true and lasting value can be found only in the actual world of change and process. When the speaker attempts to find some unchanging truth and beauty in 'Ode on a Grecian Urn', for example, he ultimately recognises that the enduring perfection of this 'Cold Pastoral' (line 45) is deathlike; it offers no change, no movement, no fulfilment. At the centre of Keats's mature vision is the paradox that an awareness of mortality increases one's sense of beauty and joy. Mortal life becomes more

> **CONTEXT**
>
> At Guy's, dissection of the human body was an integral part of training. Bodies were acquired illegally, sometimes robbed from graves, and arrived at the hospital where the young apprentices carved 'limbs and bodies, in all stages of putrefaction, & of all colours; black, green, yellow, blue' - William Osler, 'John Keats: Poet and Physician', *Journal of the American Medical Association*, 224 (1973), p.52.

**CHECK THE BOOK**

Some Romantic poets, like Coleridge, did try to distinguish 'Imagination' from other faculties of the mind, like 'Fancy'. See Chapters 13 and 14 of Samuel Taylor Coleridge's *Biographia Literaria* (1817).

valued the more one experiences its fragility and transience. Furthermore, for the later Keats, a poet who has not achieved an awareness and understanding of the dark realities of life cannot be an adequate spiritual physician. The very fact of change becomes an essential part of his eventual belief in purposeful growth.

## IMAGINATION AND TRANSCENDENCE

Keats, unlike many of the other **Romantic** poets, never formulated his ideas on the imagination in a systematic manner; his letters are nevertheless full of what he would call his 'speculations' on the workings of the imagination. One of Keats's most important discussions in this respect can be found in a letter of 22 November 1817 in which he responds to Benjamin Bailey's doubts about the authenticity of the imagination. Keats writes:

> I am certain of nothing but of the holiness of the Heart's affections and the truth of Imagination – What the imagination seizes as Beauty must be truth – whether it existed before or not – for I have the same Idea of all our Passions as of Love they are all in their sublime, creative of essential Beauty – In a Word, you may know my favourite Speculation by my first Book... The Imagination may be compared to Adam's dream – he awoke and found it truth. (*Letters* 1, p. 185).

Adam dreams that Eve has been created and awakens to find her present. What Keats suggests in this letter is that there is similarly some essential unchanging beauty and truth which can be accessed through the imagination, which works like Adam's dream. The imagination provides, as he explains further to Bailey, '"a Vision in the form of Youth" a Shadow of reality to come' (*Letters* 1, p. 185). We shall 'enjoy ourselves hereafter,' he suggests, 'by having what we called happiness on Earth repeated in a finer tone and so repeated ... Imagination and its empyreal reflection is the same as human Life and its spiritual repetition' (*Letters* 1, p. 185). The imagination provides a link between the real and the ideal. It allows us to transcend our 'mortal bars', to have a transcendent vision of the joys of immortal existence. This idea is poetically worked out in the early *Endymion*, where beauty is seen as the sensuous sign of some ultimate truth.

In the mature Keats, however, the treatment of the imagination is often more complex. The opposition between the permanence that can be reached through the imaginative vision and the transience endemic to the human condition forms the basic structuring principle of some of Keats's most celebrated poems, including 'Ode on a Grecian Urn' and 'Ode to a Nightingale'. However, what the imaginative vision can attain is not, in such poems as these, always seen as positive. Indeed, the idea that transcendent experience is debilitating, is a cheat, is a pervasive theme, and the poems repeatedly reveal the movement from vision to loss, from rapture to disillusion. Even as early as *Endymion*, it is possible to detect hints of the illusory nature of transcendent vision. While true beauty, he says in the opening to *Endymion*, binds us to the earth, transcendent vision, when it fades, makes human life all the more unbearable by emphasising the despair and confinement of the human condition. 'Lamia' can be read as demonstrating two irreconcilable ideas which reveal Keats's ambivalence about the imagination. Here the imagination, as embodied by Lamia's magical palace, gives access to something beautiful which is threatened by the public world of fact and duty. At the same time the imagination is shown as dangerous because it tempts us away from this world. There is a similar problem in 'The Eve of St Agnes'. Madeline dreams of Porphyro and awakens to find him present. This could be seen as a poetic version of that transition from dream to reality that Keats outlines in his description of Adam's dream. Alternatively imagination can be seen as colluding with Porphyro to deceive Madeline. As Jack Stillinger has pointed out, Madeline is not exactly pleased when she awakens to find Porphyro in her bed. Furthermore, in a sense there is not a straight enactment but a reversal of Keats's sequence. While he claims that 'Imagination and its empyreal reflection is the same as human Life and its spiritual repetition', in this poem the imaginative enactment of pleasure, spiritual pleasure, comes first; the earthly repetition of this is what follows – and perhaps not in a 'finer tone'.

The pattern of reversal and return found in many of the odes, particularly 'Ode to a Nightingale' and 'Ode on a Grecian Urn', also complicates the question of the imagination. In 'Ode to a Nightingale' the speaker imagines joining the nightingale 'on the

 **QUESTION**

One of the most notable characteristics of Keats's poetry is its highly concrete as opposed to abstract nature. Consider this statement with reference to three of his odes.

viewless wings of Poesy'(line 33). Poetry, imaginative vision, is posited as something magical that can transcend the human condition, transcend history itself. 'No hungry generations tread thee down' (line 62), the speaker observes of the 'immortal Bird' (line 61)

> The voice I heard this passing night was heard
> In ancient days by emperor and clown:
> Perhaps the self-same song that found a path
> Through the sad heart of Ruth, when, sick for home,
> She stood in tears amid the alien corn
>
> (lines 62–7).

But there is some danger here, and the idea of 'faery lands forlorn' (line 70) that he reaches at the conclusion of the stanza brings to the forefront an anxiety which runs through the poem. Imaginative vision may be an evasion of the real world and imaginative transformation a cheat, a deception. The real may not have been transformed or historical change and process escaped by means of the fancy; they may simply have been evaded.

## A LIFE OF SENSATIONS

**QUESTION**

'O for a Life of Sensations rather than of Thoughts!' Keats writes to his friend Benjamin Bailey. What do you think he meant? Discuss with reference to a selection of his poems.

In the letter to Bailey concerning the imagination and Adam's dream, Keats also writes: 'O for a Life of Sensations rather than of Thoughts!' (*Letters* 1, p. 185) While this exclamation has in the past been quoted out of context to support the view that Keats was a mindless sensualist, it is in fact a further refinement on Keats's early ideas concerning the Imagination, a version of Platonic idealism. For Keats sensation is, on one level, the literal information of the senses. His imagination is highly sensual: literal sensations – tastes, smells, sounds, feelings – are the basis of the powerful and condensed images of his poems. Early poems like *Endymion* suggest that it is through working on earthly sensations and passions that the imagination prefigures a transcendent world, that 'reality to come' (*Letters* 1, p. 185). Shelley's questing poet in *Alastor*, seeking the realisation of his vision of ideal beauty, ends his hopeless quest in death; Keats's questor, conversely, discovers that the way to the ideal is through the real, through the world of the senses. There is, then, a link suggested between the real and the ideal.

## BEAUTY AND TRUTH

In early poems such as *Endymion*, we find the belief that beauty must be the sensuous and temporal manifestation of some ultimate transcendent truth, some truth that gives meaning to the world of experience. Keats's growing awareness of evil and suffering gradually undermined this conviction, and beauty and truth become severed. Some of the odes look back upon this early belief with both scepticism and nostalgia. In 'Ode on Melancholy', however, Beauty is no longer the sign of some essential truth but simply one of many aspects of a contradictory reality. In 'The Fall of Hyperion' the link between beauty and truth has been completely dissolved. Now, rather than beauty, it is knowledge for which the poet seeks.

## NEGATIVE CAPABILITY

In a letter to his brothers in December 1817, Keats describes the quality that he regarded as essential to the creative mind:

> at once it struck me, what quality went to form a Man of Achievement especially in Literature & which Shakespeare possessed so enormously – I mean Negative Capability, that is when man is capable of being in uncertainties, Mysteries, doubts, without any irritable reaching after fact & reason – Coleridge, for instance, would let go by a fine isolated verisimilitude caught from the Penetralium of mystery from being incapable of remaining content with half knowledge. (*Letters* 1, p. 45)

The concept of negative capability has been taken by some critics as a definitive statement of Keats's poetics, as the idea at the heart of his own achievement. Others, however, suggest that while it is a useful concept to consider in exploring his early views, it is just one of many answers Keats posited throughout his life in his exploration of the poetic processes. The early poems may indeed show us a poet exhilarated by the freedom of doubts, uncertainties and mysteries, but much of the later poetry, including 'The Fall of Hyperion', presents a yearning for the comforts of certainties with a narrator tortured by the fear that his 'speculations' may be useless illusions. The desire for imaginative transcendence has been replaced by a desire to focus on the truth of human suffering. Rather than a concern with a 'reality to come', there is more concern for the here

**CONTEXT**

'Negative capability' is the ability to contemplate the world without the desire to try to reconcile its contradictory aspects, or fit it into closed and rational systems.

and now. The poet, like the physician, is seen to have a duty to serve suffering humanity: 'a poet is a sage; / A humanist, Physician to all men' (Canto 1, lines 189–90). Here, rather than a celebration of uncertainty, there is the agony of ignorance.

## THE 'CAMELION POET' AND THE 'EGOTISTICAL SUBLIME'

In a letter to Benjamin Bailey on 22 November 1817, Keats distinguishes between 'men of genius' and 'men of power': 'Men of Genius', he writes, 'are great as certain ethereal Chemicals operating on the Mass of neutral intellect – but they have not any individuality, any determined Character. I would call the top and head of those who have a proper self Men of Power' (*Letters* 1, p. 184). A clearer understanding of what Keats had in mind can be obtained by comparing his views on the 'camelion Poet' and the 'egotistical sublime'. The notion of the 'camelion Poet' is based on the assumption that poetry should emerge from disinterested, amoral, selfless contemplation. In a letter to Richard Woodhouse dated 27 October 1818, Keats wrote:

> A Poet is the most unpoetical of any thing in existence; because he has no Identity – he is continually in for – and filling some other Body – The Sun, the Moon, the Sea and Men and Women who are creatures of impulse are poetical and have about them an unchangeable attribute – the poet has none; no identity – he is certainly the most unpoetical of all God's Creatures (*Letters* 1, p. 386–7).

This idea of the 'camelion Poet' who is absent from his work is often linked by the critics to the idea of negative capability, and can be seen in opposition to the poet of the 'wordsworthian or egotistical sublime'. 'Poetry', Keats observes to Reynolds in a letter dated 3 February 1818:

> should be great and unobtrusive, a thing which enters into one's soul, and does not startle it or amaze it with itself but with its subject. – How beautiful are the retired flowers! How they would lose their beauty were they to throng into the highway crying out, 'admire me should be great and unobtrusive, a thing which enters into one's soul, and does not startle it or amaze it with itself but with its subject. – How beautiful are the retired

**CONTEXT**

By the term 'egotistical sublime', Keats is referring to poets who attempt to force their own philosophy upon the reader, using their imagination to modify and create, and allow the self to obtrude upon the poetry.

flowers! how they would lose their beauty were they to throng into the I am a violet! dote upon me I am a primrose!'

Keats considers Wordsworth and the modern poets generally, as opposed to those of the times of Shakespeare and Milton, much like these presumptuous flowers: 'for the sake of a few fine imaginative or domestic passages', 'are we to be bullied into a certain Philosophy engendered in the whims of an Egotist' (*Letters* 1, p. 223–5).

A knowledge of these speculations about negative capability, the 'camelion Poet' and the 'egotistical sublime' can be useful in approaching many of Keats's poems about the nature of poetry and the poet. Some critics would say that Hyperion, for example, may be seen as the 'man of power' or poet of the 'egotistical sublime' while Apollo may be seen as the man of genius or 'camelion Poet'. What evidence is there for this? Keats's odes can also be read as a series of meditations on the creative process. Paying particular attention to their typical movement of imaginative engagement and disengagement, try to relate these odes to Keats's speculations in his letters. Looking specifically at 'Ode on a Grecian Urn' and 'Ode to a Nightingale', consider what he might be saying in these poems about negative capability and the 'camelion Poet'.

**CHECK THE NET**
See West's *Death on the Pale Horse* at http://www. apocalyptic-theories. com/gallery/ horsemen/ westhorse.html.

## INTENSITY

Intensity is another key term in Keats's speculations about poetry. In the letter containing the famous statement about negative capability, he also examines this concept through a comparison between Shakespeare's *King Lear* and a painting he had recently viewed by Benjamin West entitled *Death on the Pale Horse*. The painting, he wrote,

is a wonderful picture … But there is nothing to be intense upon; no women one feels mad to kiss; no face swelling into reality. the excellence of every Art is its intensity, capable of making all disagreeables evaporate, from their being in close relationship with Beauty and Truth – Examine King Lear & you will find this exemplified throughout; but in this picture we have unpleasantness without any momentous depth of speculation excited, in which to bury its repulsiveness (*Letters* 1, p. 192).

Keats uses 'intensity' in a similar manner in the 'Pleasure Thermometer' passage of *Endymion*, Book 1:

> … But there are
> Richer entanglements, enthralments far
> More self-destroying, leading, by degrees,
> To the chief intensity: the crown of these
> Is made of love and friendship
>
> (Book 1, lines 797–801)

The thermometer, which measures heat, here provides Keats with a **metaphor** to describe the various levels of pleasure. As the degree of heat intensifies, the amount of 'self' destroyed increases and the more 'disagreeables' – in this context selfish propensities – are evaporated. Art, like heat, is capable of evaporating disagreeables, and beauty and truth, as the letter to West suggests, act as catalysts, until only the essence of the object remains. We can, perhaps, see this transformative power in operation in 'Isabella': the power of Isabella's imagination to transform reality is embodied in the basil plant: beauty grows out of horror. In the 'Ode on Melancholy' it is intensity, the glutting of sorrow on a rose, the contemplation of beauty that must die, which turns melancholy into an aesthetic experience.

There seems to have been some crisis in Keats's thought concerning intensity during 1818. In the 'Epistle to John Hamilton Reynolds' Keats relates a vision of the destructive violence of the natural world. He sees too intensely, 'Too far into the sea', into the 'core / Of an eternal fierce destruction' (lines 94–7):

> Still do I that fierce destruction see –
> The shark at savage prey, the hawk at pounce,
> The gentle robin, like a pard or ounce,
> Ravening a worm.
>
> (lines 102–5)

The imagination can see the violence of the world, but cannot understand it. Intensity can no longer make disagreeables evaporate; instead, the awareness imagination brings may be too much, may prove disabling.

**CONTEXT**

Sir Richard Burton's *Anatomy of Melancholy*, which Keats had been reading at the time he was writing 'Ode on Melancholy', recommended full indulgence in melancholic moods.

## EMPATHY

The 'camelion Poet' has the capacity for self-forgetfulness and for empathy, that is, strong sympathetic imagination which entails being taken completely up into something other to the self. 'If a Sparrow come before my Window', Keats wrote to Benjamin Bailey, 'I take part in its existence and pick about the Gravel' (*Letters* 1, p. 186). Imaginative experience begins with experience of the sensual world, such as the song of a nightingale, and develops into sensuous empathy. Such empathy, however, was not without its problems for Keats. As he recognises in such poems as 'Ode to a Nightingale', empathy can rob us of any agency, of the idea of a coherent self. The speaker recognises that complete empathetic identity with the bird deprives him of personal existence, and the desire for imaginative transcendence comes into conflict with the desire to retain self-awareness.

## KNOWLEDGE AND IDENTITY

Keats's early aesthetic ideal of negative capability gradually gave way in his poetry to the recognition of a need for knowledge and for a stable identity formed and disciplined by experience. Two much-quoted letters are of particular interest in this respect. The first, a letter to J.H. Reynolds of 3 May 1818, elaborates the simile of human life as a 'large Mansion of Many Apartments'. The first apartment is 'the infant or thoughtless Chamber, in which we remain as long as we do not think'. The second is the 'Chamber of Maiden-Thought'. In this chamber we are first intoxicated with pleasant wonders, but as the vision gradually sharpens there is a fall into self-consciousness. We become aware that 'the World is full of Misery and Heartbreak, Pain, Sickness and oppression' and this chamber 'becomes gradually darken'd'. Many doors are open, but all lead to dark passages: 'We see not the ballance of good and evil. We are in a Mist …'. The third chamber, which as Keats says presently lies beyond him, 'shall be a lucky and a gentle one – stored with the wine of love – and the Bread of Friendship'. (*Letters* 1, p. 280–3). Keats seems to have moved away now from the earlier 'O for a life of Sensation'; sensations are no longer enough: 'An extensive knowledge is needful to thinking people' (*Letters* 1, p. 277).

---

**CONTEXT**

The Pre-Raphaelites were a group of artists in the mid-Victorian age, including John Millais, Holman Hunt and Dante Gabriel Rossetti, who aimed to return to the truthfulness and simplicity of medieval art. Many of the Pre-Raphaelites admired Keats's work and painted scenes from such poems as 'Isabella' and 'The Eve of St Agnes'. See Millais' painting of 'Lorenzo and Isabella' at the Walker Art Gallery: http://www.the walker.org.uk.

A deep awareness of the world's 'Misery and Heartbreak' is seen as
a necessity for the true poet and is one of the main themes of
*Hyperion* and 'The Fall of Hyperion'. In the earlier poem Apollo
becomes a god and a true poet through 'knowledge enormous'
(Book 3, line 113), through comprehension of historical process
and the suffering endemic to the human condition. In the later
poem the questing poet must learn a similar lesson through the
tragic vision of Moneta.

A kind of sequel to the thinking in this letter is provided in the
letter to George Keats of 21 April 1819. Here Keats renounces any
idea of perfectability: 'the nature of the world', he says, 'will not
admit of it' (*Letters* 2, p. 101). Rejecting the common view of the
world as a 'vale of tears' from which 'we are to be redeemed by a
certain arbitrary interposition of God and taken to Heaven' (*Letters*
2, p. 101–2), he outlines his alternative parable of the world as 'The
vale of Soul-making'. Whereas the main point in his idea about
negative capability was the poet's lack of any specific identity, here
Keats focuses on the need for experience in order to form identity,
or 'soul': 'I say "*Soul making*" Soul as distinguished from an
Intelligence – There may be intelligences or sparks of the divinity in
millions – but they are not Souls till they acquire identities, till each
one is personally itself' (*Letters* 2, p. 102). Mutability is now seen by
Keats in a far more positive light: change is essential for
development, and identity, for Keats, is always now in process,
never complete. 'The Fall of Hyperion' is Keats's final attempt to
discover his own poetic identity, and here the poet-narrator seems
to be debating different roles. Attempt to identify these roles and
relate them to comments Keats makes in his letters. Do the various
attempts to define the poet and separate him from the dreamer lead
to any satisfactory conclusion? Has the speaker achieved any sense
of fixed identity when the poem concludes?

## WOMEN

In a letter to Benjamin Bailey, Keats describes himself as harbouring
with regard to women, 'a gordian complication of feelings, which
must take time to unravell' and 'care to keep unravelled' (*Letters* 1,
pp 341–2). This 'gordian complication of feelings' can certainly be
detected in his poems. On the one hand, as Susan Wolfson and other
critics have noted, Keats frequently uses an encounter with a female

**CHECK
THE BOOK**

For a pioneering
discussion on Keats
and gender, see
Susan Wolfson's
'Feminising Keats',
in Peter Kitson (ed.),
*New Casebooks:
Coleridge, Keats,
and Shelley*,
Macmillan 1996.

figure to represent visionary experience. On the other hand, his deepest anxieties are revealed through confrontations with power represented in a female form. The effect of the female figure upon the male in Keats's poetry is frequently described with the use of such terms as 'enthrall' or 'ensnare', simultaneously suggesting both attraction and fear. Even the letters to Fanny Brawne, while full of expressions of the intensity of his love, contain a sense of this anxiety. Telling her of his 'unalloy'd Happiness' while staying on the Isle of Wight, for example, he writes that the remembrance of her nevertheless weighs heavily upon him: 'Ask yourself my love whether you are not very cruel to have so entrammelled me, so destroyed my freedom' (*Letters* 2, p. 123).

His ambivalent attitudes towards women demonstrate quite clearly one of the ways in which Keats was very much a man of his time. In one letter, for example, Keats declares 'the generallity of women appear ... children to whom I would rather give a Sugar Plum than my time' (*Letters* 1, p. 404), and in another adds that he will not spend 'any time with Ladies unless they are handsome' (*Letters* 2, p. 20). Consider the two main female figures in 'Ode on Melancholy'. The speaker encourages the viewing and controlling of the mistress's anger: this could be said to deny her subjectivity and appropriate her as a resource for aesthetic experience. At the end of the poem, however, it is a feminised 'Veil'd Melancholy' who is empowered, and the speaker himself appropriated as a 'cloudy trophy' which magnifies this power.

Compare the relationships between the questing male figure and the visionary female figure in some of the earlier and later poems, particularly those in which poetic identity is a major concern. In the earliest poems, most notably *Endymion*, Keats's imagination often focuses on erotic encounters with a sensuous goddess or nymphs.

By the time we reach 'The Fall of Hyperion', however, the guiding goddess has become desexualised and crucial to the development of the poet-narrator. What might this suggest about the development of Keats's poetic thought? What are the gender assumptions underlying this pattern whereby the male is the quester, and what role does the female play? Note the specific occasions when Keats seem to sympathise with or admire women and when he is hostile, and try to determine what qualities or events prompt these reactions.

 **QUESTION**

Some of Keats's deepest anxieties are revealed through confrontations with power represented in a female form. What anxieties might be revealed in 'La Belle Dame sans Merci'?

It has been argued that in the earlier poems the temptation to escape the responsibility of adulthood is projected on to an entrapping female. Keats's recognition that this temptation must be resisted is in turn suggested by the way he punishes his male lovers, leaving them forlorn. Consider the way this theme works in 'La Belle Dame sans Merci' and the variation played upon the theme in 'Lamia', where the woman is not only seen as a temptation to leave the world of duty and responsibility but is also destroyed by this world. Why would it be significant that Lamia's concealed identity is that of a serpent?

Such an approach also offers an interesting perspective on many of the poems in which, while there is no actual woman, mortal or goddess, there are nevertheless abstract qualities or neutral things which Keats genders feminine. Why is Romance in 'On sitting down to read King Lear once again' feminised, addressed as a siren and queen; why in 'Ode to a Nightingale' does Keats represent the nightingale as a 'light-winged Dryad' (line 7), that is, a tree nymph? 'Ode on a Grecian Urn' has been considered particularly interesting for the way it defines and structures femininity. The urn itself is a 'still unravish'd bride of quietness' (line 1). Static and silent throughout, it is defined by the active male poet and serves as the object of his contemplation and the focus of both his desires and anxieties. The figures depicted on the urn reflect the male/female relationship established for poet and urn. The male figures, 'men or gods' (line 8) are most active, engaged in 'mad pursuit'; the women, like the urn, are static, frozen, or, at best, they 'struggle to escape' (line 9). Masculine aggression is represented as 'wild ecstasy' (line 10); is there any such ecstasy or desire presented in the female figures? What is represented in feminine and masculine terms in the description of the sacrifice. Why is this ritual so gender specific? Examining gendered representations is one way of attempting a historical and political reading of Keats's work. This kind of analysis can alert us to the ways in which Keats participated in the power relations of his time.

## ROMANCE

Romance as a genre first developed in twelfth-century France. Romance typically deals with a sophisticated courtly world of chivalry; it concerns questing knights, tournaments, magic and maidens; it is an enchanted world of marvels and wonders. Many of

**CHECK THE BOOK**

For a fuller analysis of the patriarchal assumptions implicit in 'Ode on a Grecian Urn', see Daniel P. Watkins's materialist feminist critique in 'Historical Amnesia and Patriarchal Morality', in *Spirits of Fire. English Romantic Writers and Contemporary Historical Methods*, 1990.

the tales have a strong moral content, establishing codes and ideals of chivalric behaviour. As the snowy nymphs, succulent goddesses and kisses or 'slippery blisses' (Book 2, line 741) of Endymion's bower world most clearly show, the early Keats was attracted to romance, not only the genre, but also the more general qualities associated with romance, the exotic, the idealised, and the marvellous, all qualities which encouraged an escape from the everyday world in which we live.

The main debate amongst the critics with respect to this topic has been whether Keats later repudiates romance or whether there is a continuing dialectical struggle throughout Keats's work between romance and antiromance, a struggle that could be seen to reflect his apparent ambivalence concerning the imagination. The key moment for both groups of critics is the sonnet 'On sitting down to read King Lear once again'. The notes provided on this poem should allow you to decide your own position on this issue (see **Commentaries**). You may decide there is ample evidence to support both sides of the argument. Keep in mind that it was *after* he completed this sonnet that he decided to subtitle *Endymion* 'A Poetic Romance'.

We certainly could not claim that Keats banishes romance from his work entirely. 'The Eve of St Agnes' is one clear example of a later 'romance'. 'Isabella' has been described as translating the gentleness of old romance into 'wormy circumstance' (line 385). The question which remains is: does Keats remain ambivalent about romance or does he become sceptical, antiromantic? Whichever position we take, we can say that Keats continues to exploit his ambivalence or scepticism about romance and makes it the subject of much of his poetry.

## BOWERS

The bower world of romance in which the early Keats revels, a world of sentiment, luxuriant ease and delicate beauty, is also what the early critics considered to be a world of feminine sensuousness and one of the main reasons that they saw in him a 'feminine' sensibility. Keats's obsession with the green enclosed and sheltered space of the bower where poetic and erotic activity merge has been seen to suggest romantic escapism. Keats seems to have been quite aware he was

> **CONTEXT**
>
> Early English examples of romance include the late fourteenth-century *Sir Gawain and the Green Knight*, Malory's *Le Morte d'Arthur* (1485), and Spenser's *The Faerie Queene* (1590, 1596); a notable later example is Tennyson's *Idylls of the King* (1842–85).

BOWERS continued

indulging himself here. The early Keats recognises that there is another world with which he needs to engage outside this bower: the harsh world of action and strife, a world devoid of illusions, the world of the 'masculine'. As he says in 'Sleep and Poetry'

> And can I ever bid these joys farewell?
> Yes, I must pass them for a nobler life,
> Where I may find the agonies, the strife
> Of human hearts ...
>
> (lines 122–5)

But, his immediate return to the more pleasurable 'joys' suggests, not yet.

The notion of some – at least mental – bower appears to remain attractive to Keats throughout his life; there is, for example, the fane he promises to build his goddess within his mind in the 'Ode to Psyche'. Another bower within the mind can be found in the 'Ode to a Nightingale' when he describes himself in 'embalmed darkness' (line 43) imaginatively visualising the flowers he cannot see. As Helen Vendler has noted, the tryst in this particular bower seems to be with death. How might this be significant for Keats's developing thought about such pleasurable sanctuaries far from the agony and strife of the human condition? Compare the bowers of *Endymion* with the even later 'bower' in the opening of 'The Fall of Hyperion'. How do they differ and what does this suggest about Keats's attitude towards the bower and what it represents?

## NATURE

Like the first generation Romantics Coleridge and Wordsworth, Keats, as the many bowers in his poetry suggest, found imaginative inspiration in the natural world. Unlike them, however, and probably at least partly because of his early medical training, he did not find in nature a moral guide or philosophical doctrine nor did he evoke nature as an alternative to the city. Keats tends to see nature as something cultivated and arranged for display. For him, Alan Bewell convincingly demonstrates in 'Keats's "Realm of Flora"' (*Studies in Romanticism*, 31, 1992, pp. 71–98), nature is a social product. The process of cultivation forms one of the subjects of the 'Ode to Psyche' where Keats celebrates the power of the 'gardener Fancy'(line 62). Beginning with a more Wordsworthian wild nature, full of 'dark-cluster'd trees' (line 54) and 'wild-ridged mountains' (line 55), Keats, as Bewell notes, cultivates it, turns it into a garden or park full of typically Keatsian figures like zephyrs and dryads. Then, in the midst of this he creates a 'rosy sanctuary' (line 59) full of hybrid flowers which 'never breed the same' (line 63). Keats's nature, unlike Wordsworth's, is the product of cultivation, of art.

## THE VISUAL ARTS

Ian Jack's *Keats and the Mirror of Art* has clearly demonstrated the importance of painting and sculpture to Keats. General links between his poetry and the arts can be discerned in his highly pictorial imagery. Of particular interest here is 'The Eve of St Agnes'. Keats's techniques for creating visual effects here reveal analogies with painting. More specifically, there is a frequent **iconic** element in his work: Keats often describes or responds to particular works of art, real or imaginary. There is, for example, his description of Claude's *Enchanted Castle* in the 'Epistle to J.H. Reynolds' where Keats moves away from the actual painting to include an imagined history of the castle. In this poem, as in all Keats's poems dealing with specific works, the emphasis is not so much on faithful recreation but on the examination of his responses to the art and the feelings and ideas it provokes.

Keats's main interest is in classical Greek art, and the two most important poems in this respect are 'On Seeing the Elgin Marbles' and 'Ode on a Grecian Urn'. The vogue for Greek art was begun by the German art historian Johann Winckelmann (1717–68) who wished for a recreation of the Greek spirit and the production of art according to the classical ideal of noble simplicity and calm grandeur. An English translation of his work, *Reflections on the Painting and Sculpture of Greece*, was published by J.H. Fuseli in 1765. The interest in Greek art was intensified by arrival of the Elgin Marbles in 1816, sculptures of the Parthenon purchased by Lord Elgin from the Turks. Keats wrote 'On Seeing the Elgin Marbles' after visiting the British Museum in March 1817.

'Ode on a Grecian Urn' was first published in the journal *Annals of the Fine Arts*, and in this case it is not clear whether Keats had a

**CHECK THE BOOK**

Ian Jack's *Keats and the Mirror of Art* gives convenient access to many of the paintings and sculptures significant for Keats's works. It includes forty-two plates, accompanied by analysis.

specific artwork in mind. A good place to begin an examination of Keats's responses to art in these poems is to consider Winckelmann's idealised vision of Greek art as being beyond history, as presenting a world of unchanging beauty. This clearly links to the early Keats's desire to find some eternal ideal of truth and beauty. Does he find this in the urn? He addresses his Grecian urn as a 'sylvan historian' (line 3), but does he attempt to understand it in historical terms or is he too distant from its time? Does the urn ultimately offer any historical account? Does it really represent its own time, or some fictionalised idyllic pastoral world?

# POETIC FORM AND VERSIFICATION

Keats continually experimented with a wide range of established poetic forms. He also, in the stanzas developed for his odes, designed new forms. During his short poetic career, he worked in many different genres, including lyrics, ballads, verse-epistles, odes, dream visions, epics; he drew upon all the major forms of English poetry, including Spenserian stanzas, heroic couplets, blank verse, *ottava rima*, and both Petrarchan and Shakespearean sonnet forms. The following discussion is designed to introduce just a few of the innovative aspects of Keats's experimentation with poetic form in his narrative and lyric verse.

**CONTEXT**

The Spenserian stanza was invented by Edmund Spenser for *The Faerie Queene* (1590, 1596).

## NARRATIVE VERSE

One of the main forms Keats uses for his narrative poems is the couplet or pairs of rhymed lines. What is primarily notable here is the way the early Keats resists the formal eighteenth-century style. While eighteenth-century poets exploited the epigrammatic tendency inherent in the form, Keats creates a looser and more natural flow. By using enjambment to avoid the regularity imposed by end-stopped lines, varying the placement of caesura, and introducing irregular rhythms, he breaks down the sense of each couplet being a closed unit. The differing effects achieved can be seen in a comparison of some of Keats's heroic couplets (lines of iambic pentameter rhymed in pairs) from the 'Hymn to Pan' in *Endymion* with those of the eighteenth-century poet Alexander Pope in the opening of his 'Epistle 2: (to a Lady): of the Characters of Women' (1735).

POPE:
Nothing so true as what you once let fall,
'Most Women have no Characters at all.'
Matter too soft a lasting mark to bear,
And best distinguish'd by black, brown, or fair.
How many pictures of one Nymph we view,
All how unlike each other, all how true!

(lines 1–6)

KEATS:
Thou, to whom every faun and satyr flies
For willing service, whether to surprise
The squatted hare while in half-sleeping fit;
Or upward ragged precipices flit
To save poor lambkins from the eagle's maw;
Or by mysterious enticement draw
Bewildered shepherds to their path again;

(lines 263–9)

> **CONTEXT**
>
> *Ottava rima* was used by many Italian epic poets of the Renaissance and introduced into English poetry by Wyatt.

Pope's lines have an epigrammatic quality; economy and tightness are suggested by his regular and exact rhymes and end-stopped lines; each couplet creates the sense of being a complete unit. Keats breaks down all the regularity associated with the couplet and introduces a sense of movement and energy rather than closure. This is partly the effect of his use of caesura (look for example at line 264) and partly because when a pause is required at the end of a line, Keats prefers to place this pause at the end of the *first* line of the couplet, and then run on the second line into the next couplet.

Keats experimented with a variety of other forms for narratives purposes. In 'Isabella; or The Pot of Basil' he abandoned the loose run-on couplet he had used for *Endymion*. Now dissatisfied with its effect, he turned to the much tighter and disciplined *ottava rima* stanzas consisting of eight lines of iambic pentameter, the first six rhyming alternately, the last two a rhyming couplet, *abababcc*. This is a very demanding form, and Keats's use of it shows disciplined control. Because of the 'snap' of the concluding couplet, *ottava rima* is often considered more suitable for light or satiric verse; it is the form used by Byron, for example, in *Don Juan*. While Keats worked hard to resist the epigrammatic effect of the couplet in other poetic forms, here he frequently makes that final couplet a tighter self-contained summary unit. Why is this more appropriate in this particular poem?

**QUESTION**

Many Romantic poems deal with a conflict between opposing impulses or states of being, such as innocence and experience, ideal and real, faith and doubt, aspiration and resignation. What are the major conflicts dealt with in 'Ode on a Grecian Urn' and to what extent are they resolved?

For 'The Eve of St Agnes', Keats adopted the Spenserian stanza, eight lines of iambic pentameter followed by one line of iambic hexameter (an alexandrine) and rhyming *ababbcbcc*. The interlocking rhyme scheme promotes the construction of tableaux so appropriate to Keats's highly pictorial poem, while the slow and fluid movement of the stanza and the sense of gradual lengthening in the longer last line contribute to the sensuality which marks many of the scenes he describes. In 'The Eve of St Agnes', Keats complements this implied slowness and fluidity by his use of end-stopped lines, spondaic feet and long vowels. The Spenserian stanza was used by many other Romantic poets, most notably, perhaps, Byron in *Childe Harold's Pilgrimage* (1818) and Shelley in his elegy on the death of Keats, *Adonais* (1821).

Keats wrote both his Hyperion poems in blank verse, that is, unrhymed iambic pentameter. The absence of any constraint by the rhyme scheme makes this form particularly useful for constructing the long sentences often needed for narrative verse, and allows for the development of the extended similes and catalogues frequently found in epic poetry. Blank verse was consequently a popular form for narrative, and was used by Milton in *Paradise Lost*. The Miltonic influence upon Keats's style, particularly in the first two books of *Hyperion. A Fragment*, is clear. Examples include the use of both spondees and the sixth-syllable caesura to weight and slow down the lines.

## LYRIC VERSE

In 'La Belle Dame sans Merci', Keats produced a literary ballad in which he imitated traditional ballad features. He used the traditional ballad rhyme scheme, *abcb*, but instead of alternating four- and three-stress lines, his stanza consists of three four-stressed lines with a concluding shorter line. Compare the traditional ballad stanza from 'The Douglas Tragedy' with one of Keats's stanzas:

'Rise up, rise up, now, Lord Douglas,' she says,
'And put on your armour so bright;
Let it never be said that a daughter of thine
Was married to a lord under night.'

('The Douglas Tragedy')

I made a garland for her head,
And bracelets too, and fragrant zone;
She look'd at me as she did love,
And made sweet moan.

('La Belle Dame sans Merci', lines 17–20)

A comparison shows the relative slowness and heaviness of Keats's final line as a result of the predominance of stressed syllables. Considering the effect of these final stanzaic lines in 'La Belle Dame' as a whole. Does this heaviness, as some critics have suggested, create the effect of a ghostly refrain?

Keats was clearly more interested in the sonnet than the ballad, and two fifths of his completed work is in this form. Following the example of Milton and Wordsworth, he began with the **Petrarchan** sonnet. This consists of an octave rhyming *abbaabba*, followed by a sestet, rhyming either *cdcdcd* or *cdecde*. The ideas follow the structure, with a statement of the main idea or problem in the octave, then a volta or turn to the resolution or refinement of this idea or problem within the sestet. The way in which Keats exploited the opportunities offered by this strict form is superbly demonstrated by 'On first looking into Chapman's Homer'. The idea of the poet as literary explorer is offered in the octave, the volta which prompts the turn is the discovery of Chapman's Homer, and this idea of discovery is refined in the sestet, as Keats conveys the wonder of discovery with a series of comparisons.

During 1818, Keats turned to the Shakespearean form, a move which begins with the Shakespearean ending to the Petrarchan 'On sitting down to read King Lear once again'. In the light of Keats's thematic turn from Romance to Shakespearean tragedy, this formally surprising conclusion is quite appropriate. After this, most of Keats's sonnets are in the Shakespearean form of three quatrains of alternately rhyming lines with a couplet: *ababcdcdefefgg*. An

> **CONTEXT**
>
> William Wordsworth (1770–1850) was one of the greatest of the English Romantic poets, though Keats mocked him as an example of the 'egotistical sublime'. His Petrarchan sonnets include: 'The world is too much with us; late and soon' and 'Composed upon Westminster Bridge'.

example of the way Keats followed the strict demands of this form, with the development of three successive ideas in the quatrains, may be found in 'When I have fears'. Keats tends, however, to avoid what he saw as the trivialising effect of the couplet in the Shakespearean sonnet. Examples from two of Shakespeare's sonnets demonstrate the epigrammatic nature, the sense of a grand flourish provided by the concluding couplets: 'So long as men can breathe, or eyes can see, / So long lives this, and this gives life to thee'; 'If this be error and upon me prov'd, / I never writ, nor no man ever lov'd'. In Keats's Shakespearean sonnet 'When I have fears', it becomes clear how he conversely works against this sense of a self-contained unit. To quote the couplet by itself while retaining the sense of the lines is not possible. To understand the meaning it is necessary to return back to the last quatrain and precede the couplet with the final phrase of the previous line: 'then on the shore / Of the wide world I stand alone, and think / Till love and fame to nothingness do sink' (lines 12–14).

Keats's most celebrated poems are his odes. The ode as established by the Greek poet Pindar, patterned on the dramatic chorus, was organised into three stanzas with the last in a different form from the rest. This form was adapted and developed by English poets from the seventeenth century onwards. The stanzaic structure of Keats's great odes emerges from his experiments with the sonnet form. With the exception of the first, 'To Psyche', which has a loose Pindaric form and is quite irregular in both rhyme and metre, the odes use a ten-line stanza which usually combines a Shakespearean quatrain, rhyming *abab* with a Petrarchan sestet rhymed *cdecde*. (The stanza is lengthened to eleven lines in 'To Autumn'.) This basic form allows Keats to avoid both what he considered to be the trivialising effect of the closing Shakespearean couplet and the pouncing effect of the opening Petrarchan octave. The resulting ode stanza, unlike the sonnet from which it is derived, rounds off one thought but also leads to another; in this respect, it resembles a sonnet sequence.

In 'Ode to a Nightingale' iambic pentameter is replaced by trimeter (a line consisting of three feet) in the eighth line of each stanza, but the other odes are written consistently in iambic pentameter. Compare a stanza from 'Nightingale' with stanzas from the later

**CONTEXT**

The Greek poet Pindar established the form of the ode; he wrote his odes to celebrate the winners of the Olympic and other games.

odes and try to analyse what the differing effects are. Why might Keats have dropped the trimeter after 'Nightingale'? The increasing regularity of the stanzas is matched by increasing regularity in the lines, and these lines are more frequently end-stopped than enjambed. How does this help create an appropriate tone for these particular poems?

# LANGUAGE

One of the points often made in the past with regard to Keats's development as a poet is that he moves from a 'feminine', decorative poetry of sensual excess to a more restrained, controlled 'masculine' poetry in which adolescent erotic fantasies are superseded by mature philosophical speculations. While this assessment of his development is now sometimes contested, it is still useful to consider some of the characteristics of his language in the early and more mature work which helped give rise to such a reading.

As detailed studies of his language have demonstrated, his early work is often characterised by the use of adjectives with a 'y' ending, such as 'milky' or 'lawny'. In his later works, Keats frequently replaced adjectives with participles, a technique which results in a sense of active and concentrated energy. This is demonstrated, for example, in the description of Madeline in 'The Eve of St Agnes' as she unclasps 'her warmed jewels' (line 228) - (the final 'ed' must be pronounced as a separate syllable to understand the effect). There is frequently a sense of action in Keats's language even when he is describing something that is static. The opening stanza of 'To Autumn' demonstrates how Keats can use vital action verbs while still creating a sense of stillness (see **Extended commentaries, Text 1**).

More generally, the language of the early work has been seen, both by contemporary reviewers and some modern critics, as marked by vulgarity, lapses in good taste, a certain stylistic 'badness'. In contrast, the language of the mature work has been described as more poised, dignified and 'virile'. This mature work displays the intensity and control that Keats himself valued: in the skilful patterning of lines, the concentrated effects of his abundant images

 **CHECK THE NET**

*Romanticism on the Net* is a useful online journal that publishes articles and reviews of recent books on writers of the Romantic period. Look up **http://users.ox.ac.uk/~scat0385/.**

in which ideas are repeated, reinforced and extended. Not all critics have preferred the language of the mature work, however. Christopher Ricks locates the central Keats as the rich poet of such early works as *Endymion* and 'The Eve of St Agnes' rather than the sombre poet of such mature works as 'The Fall of Hyperion'. Admiring the verbal excesses which seem to have discomfited so many early and later critics, Ricks believes Keats's best poetry risks vulgarity and turns what might be embarrassing into something rich and disconcerting (Christopher Ricks, *Keats and Embarrassment*, Oxford University Press, 1974, pp. 7–8). He sees the Keats of the early poetry as exploring a kind of manliness which is capable of full sensual indulgence. The phrase 'slippery blisses' to describe kisses in *Endymion*, often taken as evidence of immaturity or indecency, is instead for Ricks an admirably audacious piece of writing with a liberating value for the male reader.

**CONTEXT**
Keats originally dedicated *Endymion* to the young poet, Thomas Chatterton (1752–70) who wrote a number of fake poems in the style of Ossian (a legendary Gaelic warrior and bard). Chatterton committed suicide by taking arsenic when he was eighteen years old. His life had a powerful effect on Romantic painters and writers. Keats is said to have described him as 'the purest writer in the English language'.

While is it possible to see this general evolution in Keats's poetic style, we need to be wary of oversimplifying his achievement in suggesting he moves from one kind of language to another. He draws upon various different kinds of language throughout his career. He even, most notably in the odes, changes the **registers** of diction frequently within particular poems, and we need to consider what the effect of such changes may be. Why are there changes in the language the speaker uses to address Psyche; why does he move between religious language and the language of pastoral eroticism? The austere formality of 'O Goddess' forms a striking contrast with the warm sensuality of the previous 'happy, happy dove' ('Ode to Psyche', lines 1 and 22). Similarly, in 'Ode to a Nightingale', why is death described in such luxuriantly sensuous terms; why is the nightingale first addressed familiarly as a 'light-winged Dryad' (line 7) and then reverently when the speaker declares 'Thou was not born for death, immortal Bird'(line 61)? These differences in language reveal a changing relationship between the speaker and the object of his contemplation. Similarly, consider the change that is registered when the speaker, who has previously referred to imaginative powers as 'the viewless wings of Poesy' (line 33), finally calls Fancy a 'deceiving elf' (line 74).

While Keats employs a wide variety of diction and styles, there is little chance of us confusing any of his speakers with Wordsworth's ideal of the poet who speaks in the language really used by men. One of the first identifiable characteristics in Keats's poetry is its highly literary nature. Reading Keats, we also need to be alert to his musical effects, his skilful use of sound. His stanzas are frequently bound together by a complex patterning of sound effects, including such types of repetition as assonance, alliteration, and anaphora. As an example, consider the skilful patterning in the third stanza of the 'Ode on a Grecian Urn':

**QUESTION**
Choose another stanza from 'Ode on a Grecian Urn' and analyse its sound patterns.

> Ah, happy, happy boughs! that cannot shed
> Your leaves, nor ever bid the spring adieu;
> And, happy melodist, unwearied,
> For ever piping songs for ever new;
> More happy love! more happy, happy love!
> For ever warm and still to be enjoy'd,
> For ever panting, and for ever young;
> All breathing human passion far above,
> That leaves a heart high-sorrowful and cloy'd,
> A burning forehead, and a parching tongue.
>
> (lines 21–30)

Many lines in the stanza are clearly linked through the use of the anaphoric 'For ever', emphasising the idea that what is embodied by the urn is eternal, and through the insistent repetition of 'happy'. Slightly less obviously, the alliterative 'h', 'p' and 'b' create a sense of connection in the stanza as a whole. The placement of **caesuras** creates a sense of balance while the numerous pauses suggest the speaker's delight in lingering over the scene.

The numerous rhetorical devices Keats employs are always functional stylistically and thematically. This can be demonstrated by considering the repeated questions, the insistent repetition, puns, **oxymorons**, and ambiguities of 'Ode on a Grecian Urn'. Not only do many of these create the kind of patterning previously discussed, in addition, they can be said to create within the reader the same kind of doubts experienced by the poet's speaker. As the poet is struggling to understand how to interpret the urn, so we struggle to understand how to interpret the poem: our doubts and questions reflect his.

# IMAGERY

Keats is generally considered to be a master of the image, and it would probably be difficult to name one type of image that he does not, at some point, use. In discussing the general qualities of his imagery, however, we could say that it is marked by five main characteristics which will be discussed in turn. They are:

concrete
pictorial
compressed
associational
synaesthetic

## CONCRETE

**CHECK
THE BOOK**
Detailed close
readings of Keats's
odes can be found
in Helen Vendler's
*The Odes of John
Keats* (1983).

Perhaps the most notable characteristics of Keats's poetry is its highly concrete, as opposed to abstract, nature. It is certainly possible to find examples of abstract terms in his work; the well-known lines at the opening of *Endymion* are composed entirely of abstract ideas: 'A thing of beauty is a joy for ever: Its loveliness increases; it will never / Pass into nothingness' (Book 1, lines 1–3). More typically, however, Keats conveys such abstract ideas through tangible, material forms. A striking example may be found in the lines describing the landscape and the fallen Saturn at the beginning of 'Hyperion':

> Deep in the shady sadness of a vale
> Far sunken from the healthy breath of morn,
> Far from the fiery noon, and eve's one star,
> Sat gray-hair'd Saturn, quiet as a stone,
> Still as the silence round about his lair;
> Forest on forest hung about his head
> Like cloud on cloud. No stir of air was there,
> Not so much life as on a summer's day
> Robs not one light seed from the feather'd grass,
> But where the dead leaf fell, there did it rest.
> A stream went voiceless by, still deadened more
> by reason of his fallen divinity
> Spreading a shade: the Naiad 'mid her reeds
> Press'd her cold finger closer to her lips.
>
> (Book 1, lines 1–14)

Keats creates a scene of extraordinary oppression, stillness and silence which ominously conveys Saturn's loss of power and creativity. The abstract quality of 'sadness' is given concrete form by the accompanying adjective 'shady', and the abstract quality of 'quiet' by the simile 'as a stone'. The suffocating sense of gloom and impotence becomes tangible as the dead leaf falls to rest and the stream goes silently by, while the overwhelming sense of numbness and cold is given substance by the final description of the Naiad who presses 'her cold finger closer to her lips'.

## PICTORIAL IMAGERY

Closely linked to Keats's concern with the concrete is his tendency towards pictorial imagery. Ideas, as the previously quoted example of the Naiad demonstrates, are frequently presented in an intensely visual form. Personification is one of the many techniques Keats uses to create this pictorial effect. In the 'Ode on Melancholy', for example, a series of such abstractions as Beauty and Pleasure are personified; they become vital figures that can actually be envisioned. A striking example is the figure of 'Joy, whose hand is ever at his lips / Bidding adieu' (lines 22-3). 'The Eve of St Agnes' has been particularly admired for its pictorial qualities (see discussion in **Commentaries**).

## COMPRESSION

There is also a remarkable compression of meaning in Keats's images. Consider the effect of such condensed images from the odes as '*alien* corn' and '*aching* Pleasure'. Look at these lines from *Endymion*:

> ... Here is wine,
> Alive with sparkles – never, I aver,
> Since Ariadne was a vintager,
> So cool a purple ...

> (Book 2, lines 441–4)

Coolness is here used to modify purple, and therefore to suggest delight in the beauty of the colour, but purple is also a **metonymic** image for the wine and so can be taken to suggest delight in its chill.

> **QUESTION**
> How does Keats exploit pictorial imagery in 'To Autumn'?

## SYNAESTHESIA

The fusion of the visual and the tactile in this last example leads to another characteristic of Keats's imagery, the frequent use of synaesthesia, or the substitution of one sense for another. Simple examples would include the Titans sitting in 'pale and silver silence' in *Hyperion* (Book 2, line 356) or Lamia in the process of transformation from serpent to woman, writhing in 'scarlet pain' (Part 1, line 154). Where we expect a sound image to describe silence, and a tactile image to describe pain, we are instead given visual images. More typical of Keats, however, is a complex use of this device whereby several diverse sense-impressions are brought together in order to convey his perception of an object. Hyperion's palace door is described with a mingling of touch, sight, and smell: 'like a rose in vermeil tint and shape, / In fragrance soft, and coolness to the eye' (*Hyperion* Book 1, lines 209–210). Similarly, when the speaker of 'Ode to a Nightingale' imaginatively reaches the world of the nightingale in stanza 5, he is in 'embalmed darkness' and cannot see the flowers at his feet or 'what soft incense hangs upon the boughs'. The sense of smell that we typically link to our experience of flowers is suggested by 'incense'. This scent, however, is substantiated, deepened, by the word 'soft', which suggests not what we might feel if we could touch the actual blossoms in the trees but what we might feel if we could touch their scent. Keats's use of synaesthesia here is a strong assertion of the imagination's power to see and feel more than the sensory eye can literally see, its power to feel more than what is literally touchable.

> **? QUESTION**
> Can you find examples of synaesthesia in 'Ode on a Grecian Urn'?

## ASSOCIATIONAL IMAGERY

To attempt to explain and transcribe the literal meaning of many of Keats's images is problematic since they frequently work through association. This is particularly notable in the imagery of the second stanza in 'Ode to a Nightingale':

> O, for a draught of vintage! that hath been
> Cool'd a long age in the deep-delved earth,
> Tasting of Flora and the country green,
> Dance, and Provençal song, and sunburnt mirth!
> O for a beaker full of the warm South,

> Full of the true, the blushful Hippocrene,
> With beaded bubbles winking at the brim,
> And purple-stained mouth

The stanza in fact provides an excellent example of all the tendencies in Keats's imagery. The images are highly concrete and pictorial. Those last three lines do not suggest only the taste of the wine – its bubbles breaking on the lips – they also make this taste tangible by conjuring up the picture of a slightly intoxicated satyr – or perhaps Dionysus himself – participating in some bacchic revel, his mouth stained with wine, his eyes rather blearily winking. The stanza also reveals an intense compression of imagery: 'sunburnt mirth', for example, conveys through just two words the joyful celebrations of happy countryfolk, bronzed by the sun. It is complexly synaesthetic. He calls for a taste of wine which he describes in terms of other senses: the visual in the 'country green', the aural in 'Provençal song' and the tactile 'the warm South'. Finally, the images here work by association. The taste of the wine he imagines is first associated with Flora and the green countryside and this leads Keats on to dance and song and laughter. Clearly, it would be difficult to explain how anything could literally taste of such things; it is the sense of innocent and carefree pleasure that they evoke which Keats is associating with the taste of the wine.

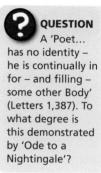

**QUESTION**
A 'Poet... has no identity – he is continually in for – and filling – some other Body' (Letters 1,387). To what degree is this demonstrated by 'Ode to a Nightingale'?

# PART FOUR

## CRITICAL HISTORY

# 'SNUFF'D OUT BY AN ARTICLE'

An 1848 review in the *New Monthly Magazine* concisely summarises the critical responses of Keats's contemporaries to his work:

> It was the misfortune of Keats as a poet, to be either extravagantly praised or unmercifully condemned. The former had its origin in the generous partialities of friendship, somewhat obtrusively displayed; the latter in some degree, to resentment of that friendship, connected as it was with party politics, and peculiar views of society as well as of poetry (qtd in Matthews, p. 1).

While favourable reviews of Keats's work were written, often by his friends, these were far outnumbered by dismissive and frequently vicious attacks. These attacks were motivated by political as much as by aesthetic considerations. They were at least partly the result of Keats's friendship with the radical poet Leigh Hunt, who promoted the work of both Keats and Shelley in his weekly paper *The Examiner*.

The most damaging attacks on Keats's poetry came in John Wilson Croker's review of *Endymion* in the *Quarterly Review* and John Gibson Lockhart's 1818 review of *Endymion* and *Poems* (1817) in *Blackwood's Magazine*, both published anonymously as was then the custom. Lockhart's review was exceptionally malicious. Ridiculing Keats for his youth, social background, and supposed political sympathies, and dismissing *Endymion* as 'drivelling idiocy', he recommended that 'Johnny Keats', that overambitious apothecary's apprentice, would be well advised to return to his pills and plasters.

The reactions of Keats's friends and associates to the attacks of the reviewers were to have a marked influence upon later assessments of his work. They defended him by insisting upon his isolation from the political world. A poet whose poems were published and received in a highly charged political context, Keats soon became strikingly depoliticised and dehistoricised. He was considered to have little to do with the world and its concerns, and to be most at home in poetry, in the world of sense and imagery. This view of Keats was reinforced by Shelley who, on hearing of Keats's death, composed his elegy, *Adonais*. In his preface, Shelley offered a counterattack on the reviewers: 'The genius of the lamented person to whose memory I have dedicated these unworthy verses,' he wrote,

> was not less delicate and fragile than it was beautiful; and where cankerworms abound, what wonder if its young flower was blighted in the bud? The savage criticism on his *Endymion*, which appeared in the *Quarterly Review*, produced the most violent effect on his susceptible mind; the agitation thus originated ended in the rupture of a blood-vessel in the lungs; a rapid consumption ensued.

Rather ironically it was this elegy rather than any of his own works that kept the name of Keats alive for the next twenty-five years, and it was this elegy that played a key role in establishing the myth of 'poor Keats' as a sensitive and unworldly genius, a helpless victim who was destroyed by the critics – or as Byron more flippantly avers in *Don Juan* – 'snuff'd out by an article' (Canto 11, stanza 60).

## REREADING KEATS: A CHANGING VIEW

Keats had a profound influence on many writers of the nineteenth century. This influence is already evident, for example, in the early Tennyson. The Pre-Raphaelites of mid-century read him avidly and, seeing him as a poet of sensuous richness and vivid pictorial effects, frequently produced paintings which illustrated his works. Walter Pater claimed him as a forerunner of the art for art's sake movement, and by the end of the nineteenth century Keats's reputation as a major poet had been firmly established.

 **CHECK THE NET**

For an informal chatroom discussion on Keats, go to **http://federallistnavy. com /poetry/ JOHNKEATS1795- 1821hall/ wwwboard.html.**

At the beginning of the twentieth century, the view of Keats began to change, and rather than being seen only as a poet of the senses, he began to be valued for his powerful intellect, his willingness to confront the larger philosophical questions of human existence. For most of the twentieth century, nevertheless, the myth of Keats's unworldiness retained a firm hold on many critics. Even the Post-

REREADING KEATS: A CHANGING VIEW continued

**CHECK THE BOOK**

Included in Bates' collection is an important essay by Jack Stillinger who, as the title of his essay suggests, 'The Hoodwinking of Madeline: Skepticism in *The Eve of St Agnes*', argued for Keats as an antiromantic.

Structuralist Paul de Man, in his introductory remarks to his *Selected Poetry of John Keats*, appeared to confirm the apparent consensus that Keats invited formalist readings: 'In reading Keats', he wrote, we are 'reading the work of a man whose experience is mainly literary ... In this case, we are on very safe ground when we derive our understanding primarily from the work itself' (p. xi). This view of Keats made his poetry particularly attractive to the New Critics, and the formalist approach has produced some influential readings of Keats's poetry, including Cleanth Brooks's celebrated analysis of the verbal and structural effects of 'Ode on a Grecian Urn'. A useful selection of mid twentieth-century commentary on Keats can be found in Walter Jackson Bate's *Keats: A Collection of Critical Essays*.

## HISTORICISING KEATS: THE LAST TWO DECADES

Jerome McGann's attack on the dominant aesthetic traditions of Keats criticism in 'Keats and the Historical Method in Literary Criticism' (1979) was instrumental in demonstrating that Keats's poetry could be fruitfully interpreted using historicist methodologies. After McGann, it became difficult to maintain the myth of the unworldly poet. As Romantic studies generally turned towards the kind of contextually informed criticism associated with new historicism, Keats's political and social thought began to receive scholarly attention. In a 1986 special issue of *Studies in Romanticism* devoted to 'Keats and Politics' and edited by Susan Wolfson, the various contributors all agreed in seeing Keats as a radical, while offering differing assessments of how this radicalism influenced and was revealed in his work. Marjorie Levinson, in *Keats's Life of Allegory: The Origins of a Style* (1988), reads Keats's poetry in the light of the disadvantages imposed by his background, class and class. His obsession with the themes of fulfilment and anticipation, Levinson suggests, are the class obsessions of a particular section of the middle class wanting to arrive at a position of power and dominance. Daniel Watkins's *Keats's Poetry and the Politics of the Imagination* (1989) demonstrates how his poetry is, from the very start, haunted by politics. Keats appears here as a poet who embodies the historical anxieties and insecurities of his age: his 'articulation and reworking of traditional poetic topics, of myths and legends, and of contemporary and past history and politics' are all seen by Watkins as signs of the intense anxiety of 'an age threatened by economic collapse, by the militarization of culture, bad harvests, staggeringly high unemployment, and by a fear both of bourgeois, industrial triumph and of a return to feudalism' (p. 23).

The movement away from formalism prompted by historicist methodologies has recently been challenged by a number of critics who have argued that the issue of Keats's artistry has been forgotten in the attempt to rewrite him as a poet involved in political and social issues of his age. Such historicist critics as Nicholas Roe in *John Keats and the Culture of Dissent* have responded to such anxieties by offering fresh readings of the poems which re-examine Keats's artistry while simultaneously emphasising their topicality. A number of works which draw on more traditional methodologies and concentrate primarily on matters of style have also been published in the last twenty years. One of the best of these is Helen Vendler's *The Odes of John Keats*.

Other critical works of particular interest which draw on various theoretical methodologies include Andrew Bennett's *Keats, Narrative and Audience*. Bennett offers new readings of the major poems emerging out of recent theoretical discussions concerning narrative, readers and reading. Feminist discussions of Keats include Susan Wolfson's 'Feminising Keats', which provides an account of Keats's reception from the Romantic age to the present time, focusing upon the apparent obsession with his masculinity. While his admirers tend to defend his masculinity, his detractors, she shows, describe his style and manner as effeminate and ascribe to him the feminine qualities of weakness, excess and passivity. This, Wolfson suggests, is related to a more general anxiety about the feminisation of the male in the Romantic period. The gender implications of Keats's use of language have been interestingly explored by Alan J. Bewell in 'Keats's "Realm of Flora"'. Less positively, Margaret Homans's 'Keats Reading Women, Women Reading Keats' (1990) has argued that Keats equates his poetic project with male sexual potency and carries out a masculine appropriation of the feminine. Anne K. Mellor, who in *Romanticism and Gender* (1993) argues that there are two different kinds of

**CHECK THE BOOK**

For a representative sample of the critical debates generated by the Keats bicentenary in 1995, see Michael O'Neill (ed.), *Keats: Bicentenary Readings* (1997).

**CHECK THE BOOK**

Keats's attitudes towards romance are considered by Mark Sandy in 'Dream Lovers and Tragic Romance' (2000), an article in the online journal Romanticism on the Net. 20 (November 2000).

Romanticism, one 'masculine' and the other 'feminine'. Her analysis of Keats's own gender ideology as revealed in both his letters and his poetry shows him working within yet struggling against a feminine Romantic aesthetic. Mellor demonstrates how frequently Keats positioned himself within the realm of the feminine in his poetic theory, and considers the ambivalence in his attitude towards gender.

# PART FIVE

## BACKGROUND

## JOHN KEATS'S LIFE AND WORK

John Keats was born in London on 31 October 1795 into a relatively prosperous lower-middle-class family; he was the eldest child of Thomas Keats, manager of a livery stables, and Frances Jennings. His father died in 1804 after being thrown from a horse, and in 1810 his mother died from tuberculosis. Keats left school in 1811 to be apprenticed to the surgeon Thomas Hammond. After four years of apprenticeship he registered as a student at Guy's Hospital. He began writing poetry in 1814 and his first publication, the sonnet 'O Solitude', appeared in the radical weekly, *The Examiner*, on 5 May 1816. The editor, Leigh Hunt, subsequently became a friend and strong supporter of Keats, and with Hunt's encouragement Keats decided to abandon medicine and pursue a literary career. His first collection, *Poems*, appeared in 1817, followed in April of 1818 by *Endymion*. When his brother George emigrated to America, Keats took his place in looking after the youngest brother Tom, who had tuberculosis. During the summer of 1818, Keats went on a walking tour of Northern England and Scotland with his friend Charles Brown. On his return he found Tom was dying; he nursed him until he died at the end of the year. During this time Keats met Fanny Brawne and they became engaged in December 1819. His plans to marry Fanny, however, were thwarted by financial problems and illness. Frustrated by his inability to publish poetry profitably, Keats attempted two dramatic works, a five-act tragedy entitled *Otho the Great*, which was never performed, and the uncompleted *King Stephen*. The tuberculosis Keats had probably contracted while caring for his brother became active in the autumn of 1819 and he experienced severe haemorrhaging in February of 1820. The last of the three volumes of poetry published during his lifetime, *Lamia, Isabella, The Eve of St Agnes and Other Poems* appeared in July. In September of that same year, he went to Italy for the sake of his health, accompanied by his friend Joseph Severn, a painter. The journey was difficult, and his condition declined. He died, aged twenty-five, on 23 February 1821 and was buried in the Protestant Cemetery in Rome.

 **CHECK THE NET**
For a good selection of images of Keats, see http://english history.net/keats/images.html.

 **CHECK THE NET**
See the tombstone of Keats and his friend Joseph Severn at http://medpharm53.bu.edu/pages/cemeteries/cemeteries-rome.html.

## KEATS'S LETTERS

Keats's letters are among the best produced by any literary figure. His major correspondents include his brothers Tom and George and his sister Fanny; his friend Benjamin Bailey (1791–1853); Fanny Brawne (1800–1865), to whom the famous love letters are addressed; the writer Charles Armitage Brown (1786–1842); Charles Cowden Clarke (1787–1877), an early friend and literary influence; Benjamin Haydon (1786–1846), a painter whom Keats admired; and Joseph Severn (1793–1879), the impecunious artist who was with Keats when he died.

Energetic and engaging, the letters are full of spontaneity, humour and emotion. Keats constantly moves between the social and literary worlds, mixing his ideas about poetry with descriptions of things as various as dinners and parsons, freemasonry and fairy tales. The journal letter to George and Tom Keats of 21/27 December 1817 provides a good example of the wide range of topics with which he engages. He begins with a performance by the actor Edmund Kean that he has reviewed; he then moves to a discussion of Benjamin West's painting *Death on the Pale Horse* as compared to Shakespeare's *King Lear* ; this is followed with a description of dinner with Horace Smith and friends, whose company he by no means enjoyed; this in turn leads on to his famous statement about negative capability (see **Themes**); finally, Keats concludes with a brief reference to the most recent poem published by Shelley (*Letters* 1, p. 192).

**CHECK THE NET**
For a general overview of Keats's life, go to **Victorian Web. John Keats. An Overview:**http://65.107.211.206/previctorian/keats/keatsov.html.

As Keats's poetry is notably dialectical, so his letters are rarely dogmatic or conclusive but rather explorative, questioning. It is, as a result, dangerous to read these letters with the aim of determining what Keats believed; no matter what opinion is selected, it is likely that a quite different, even opposing, opinion will be entertained a few pages later. In the well-known letter to Benjamin Bailey of 22 November 1817, he declares: 'I am certain of nothing but of the holiness of the Heart's affections and the truth of Imagination' (*Letters* 1, p. 184). A few months later, however, he confesses to this same correspondent 'I have not one Idea of the truth of any of my speculations' (*Letters* 1, p. 243), and the truth of the imagination was something he certainly came to question. Nevertheless, the letters offer a great deal of insight into the personality of John Keats and, used judiciously, some help in understanding his work. Throughout this Note, references are made to letters in which Keats comments upon particular poems or ideas.

## HISTORICAL BACKGROUND

Keats lived through an era of turbulent change, an era that crucially altered Western history. A severe economic crisis had intensified social antagonisms and led to the French Revolution of 1789, the year also generally associated with the beginnings of the Romantic movement in Britain. No longer able to tolerate oppression, the working classes of France revolted, the monarchy was overthrown, and democracy and socialism began to spread throughout Europe. Although ending rather disappointingly during 1799 with a dictatorship rather than a true democracy, the French Revolution had an enormous appeal throughout Europe, and the first-generation Romantic poets enthusiastically supported this revolt against oppression. 'Bliss was it in that dawn to be alive', as Wordsworth later wrote in *The Prelude* (Book 11, line 108).

In Keats's lifetime, revolt also began to seem a distinct possibility closer to home. England was in the midst of the Industrial Revolution, the term used to describe that period of social, economic and ergonomic change generally dated from 1750 to 1830. There was a movement away from an agricultural to a manufacturing economy, and for those who worked in the factories and mills, conditions were frequently appalling. The rapid expansion of the population in the towns and cities resulted in poor housing, inadequate sanitation and widespread disease. The introduction of new technologies also threatened the livelihoods of many of the working classes, and this threat often provoked violent reactions. The Luddite disturbances of 1811–17, during which factories and mills were attacked and machines destroyed, stirred memories of the even more frightening excesses of the French Revolution. In the aftermath of the defeat of Napoleon at Waterloo, when a series of poor harvests in Britain led to legislation to keep the price of corn high, there were numerous active protest meetings and marches. People began to demand electoral reform, work

**CHECK THE NET**

For information concerning significant events during Keats's lifetime, look at http://english.ucsb. edu:591/rchrono/ and also **Voice of the Shuttle. Romantics:http:// vos.ucsb.edu/ browse. asp?id=2750.**

opportunities, better wages and lower prices. The most notorious event was that which came to be known as the 'Peterloo Massacre' of August 1819. Some 60,000 people gathered in St Peter's Fields, Manchester, in support of parliamentary reform; the local magistrates, after allowing the meeting, decided to arrest the speakers, and sent in first the constabulary, then the Yeomanry, and finally the Fifteenth Hussars, professional soldiers who were wearing the battle colours they had worn at Waterloo; the crowd was violently dispersed, eleven killed and many hundreds injured.

Keats's political stance is certainly revealed in his letters where he repeatedly expresses his abhorrence of tyranny, his sympathy with suffering and a commitment to a liberal view of history as progressive enlightenment, a continual change for the better. His general views on change and progress, as well as his more specific views on the French Revolution and its consequences for England, are outlined in a journal letter to George and Georgiana Keats written 18 September, one month after Peterloo (*Letters* 2, pp. 193–4).

**CONTEXT**

Keats's letters, however, sometimes do reveal political interest. In a letter of September 1819, he railed against the Tory government, saying that it had given 'our Court hopes of a turning back to the despotism of the 16 century…they spread a horrid superstition against all inovation (*sic*) and improvement'. They had used the French Revolution to 'undermine our freedom'.

Direct statements of Keats's political beliefs, however, are rarely found in the poems; one notable exception is the attack on the capitalist brothers in 'Isabella'. Traditionally critics have accepted the myth of Keats's unworldliness that originated during his lifetime (see **Themes**). They have considered him aloof from the events of contemporary life, the most apolitical of the Romantic poets. More recent critics have replaced this dehistoricised Keats with a politically engaged poet. Seminal in this respect is Jerome McGann's essay 'Keats and the Historical Method in Literary Criticism' (*MLN*, 91, 1979, pp. 988–1032), a convincing argument for a historically oriented criticism. Marilyn Butler's work has been equally revisionary in producing a new historicised and politicised Keats. Butler argues, for example, that the larger intention in both Hyperion poems is 'to represent historical change as the liberal habitually sees it: continuous, inevitable, and on the most universal level grand, for it is Progress – the survival of the fittest, the best, the most beautiful and the quintessentially human' (*Romantics, Rebels, and Reactionaries*, 1981, p. 151). For suggestions about further historically oriented criticism, see **Critical History**.

# LITERARY BACKGROUND

## ROMANTICISM

The Romantic period is a convenient term for describing that period
in English literary history dating from 1789, the time of the French
Revolution, to about 1830. The first generation of Romantic poets
includes Blake, Wordsworth and Coleridge; the second includes
Byron, Shelley and Keats. The 'big six', as they are often called, by
no means regarded themselves as part of a unified group.
'Romanticism' was only created as a distinct movement and object
of study in the later part of the nineteenth century. They were
actually much divided in their political, religious and artistic beliefs,
and to place Keats by, say, Byron, is to be faced with two very
different poets. Nevertheless, a number of general characteristics
might be seen as loosely characteristic of Romanticism. These
include a valuing of feeling and emotion over reason; an interest in
the investigation of the self; a new concern with nature as a means of
understanding this self; a focus on the imagination; a yearning
towards something transcendent, beyond the ordinary world; and a
rebellion against outmoded poetic and political institutions.

Keats was to a degree influenced by the first-generation Romantics,
particularly Wordsworth. He admired what he saw as Wordsworth's
ability to incorporate the miseries of the world into a transcendent
vision, but was often wary of what he called Wordsworth's
'egotistical sublime'. For Keats, the poet's function was not to
impose a vision or interpretation upon the world, as he thought
Wordsworth did, but rather to immerse and lose the self in what
was perceived (see **Themes**, on **The 'camelion Poet'**).

## OTHER LITERARY INFLUENCES

Keats is a highly literary poet in that throughout his poetic career he
echoes, appropriates and adapts for his own purposes the forms,
language, images and ideas of other writers, always, however,
remaining aware of the need to express his own poetic vision. One
of the earliest influences on the early Keats is Spenser: his first
surviving poem is the 'Imitation of Spenser', written in 1814. We can
also detect the influence of, among others, Chaucer, Shakespeare,
Dante, Scott and the Gothic novelists such as Ann Radcliffe.

 **CHECK
THE NET**
There are several
sites which will help
you fill in the
background of the
Romantic period.
Try **Literary
Resources.
Romantic:**http://
andromeda.
rutgers.edu/~jlynch
/Lit/romantic.html.

Leigh Hunt, editor of the radical journal *The Examiner*, had a significant influence on Keats's early work. Hunt and the so-called 'Cockney School' with which he was associated believed the function of poetry was primarily to provide pleasure and consequently advocated luxuriant and sensuous language and images. His influence on Keats can be most clearly seen in the 1817 volume, *Poems*, an exuberant celebration of pleasure, beauty and freedom where Keats luxuriates in description, and image enthusiastically tumbles over image.

In his more mature work, Keats also demonstrates the powerful influence of Milton. This is particularly notable in the first *Hyperion*. The influence can be seen not only in the choice of epic form, and in the focus upon a Fall, but also in the language, in the use of the adjective in place of the adverb ('Shook horrid with such aspen malady'), for example, and in such Miltonic inversions as the use of the epithet after the noun ('omens drear'). In versification Milton's influence is also clear: in the use of **spondees** to slow down and weight the lines and in the use of the sixth-syllable **caesura**. When Keats made his later attempt at revising the story in 'The Fall of Hyperion', he moved away from Milton to the Dantean dream vision. This was partly because by this point he found the Miltonic influence oppressive, and partly because the epic was no longer so popular and vision or dream poems, such as Coleridge's 'Kubla Khan: or, A Vision in a Dream' were more successful. In this second *Hyperion*, the influence of Dante, suggested also by the movement from epic books to cantos, is far more notable.

### THE HELLENIC REVIVAL

With the publication of Lord Byron's *Childe Harold's Pilgrimage* (1812), which focuses on the ruin and desired rebirth of classical glory, literary philhellenism (love of Greece) can be said to have become a widespread movement. For Keats, who shared with his fellow Romantics an admiration for the simplicity and sensuousness of the pagan world, the classical Greeks affirmed the preeminence of Art and Beauty. The Hellenic revival was, at least in part, a reaction against the dominant values and beliefs of the policy makers in Regency Britain: it is not insignificant that Book 3 of *Endymion* opens with an attack upon the 'baaing vanities' (line 3) of bishops, kings and emperors. As Marilyn Butler observes in *Romantics,*

---

**CONTEXT**

Dante Alighieri's (1265–1321) most famous work is the *Divina Commedia*, an epic poem and his spiritual testament, chronicling a journey through *Inferno* (hell) and *Purgatorio* (Purgatory) guided by Virgil, and finally by his childhood sweetheart, Beatrice. His use of vernacular Italian, rather than Latin, in a work of art was revolutionary at the time.

*Rebels, and Reactionaries*, Greek mythology provided early nineteenth-century writers with an occasion for dissent from prevailing orthodoxies.

The early Keats also uses Greek worship to suggest a natural form of religious worship, to express his own conviction of what an enlightened religion ought to be. The rites of Pan in Book 1 of *Endymion*, for example, are part of a joyful and innocent celebration, full of laughter, singing and dancing. The sacrifice offered to Pan is a bloodless one – although Keats must have known animal sacrifice to be an integral part of Greek religion. His choice of Pan as the deity of Latmos quite clearly indicates his desire to contrast the joys of this religion with the gloom of Christianity. According to the traditional story first written down by Plutarch, at the time when Christ was crucified a group of mariners heard a voice across the waters proclaiming 'The Great God Pan is dead': the birth of Christianity was the death of the pagan world. In resurrecting Pan, Keats here rejects a religion of suffering.

When Keats mentions the name of a mythical figure, even if it is just a brief reference, he assumes the reader will know the background story and therefore understand the implications of the reference. To give an example, when Lamia is described as lifting her 'Circean' head (Part I, line 115), it is useful to know that Circe was the enchantress who changed Odysseus's companions into swine. Keats's reference thereby becomes loaded with meaning: Lamia is like Circe herself in that she too is an enchantress with magical powers, but she is also like one of Circe's victims in that she has been changed from woman into serpent. The ambiguity that so notably marks her presentation is consequently suggested even by this brief metaphor.

**CHECK THE BOOK**

In reading many of Keats's poems, most notably the narratives *Endymion*, *Hyperion*, and 'The Fall of Hyperion' but also a number of the lyrics, such as 'Ode to Psyche', it is useful to consult a classical dictionary.

| Events in Europe | Author's life | Literary events |
|---|---|---|
| | | 1792 William Blake, *Song of Liberty*; Mary Wollstonecraft, *Vindication of the Rights of Women* |
| 1789-95 French Revolution | | |
| 1793 France declares war on Britain; Reign of Terror | 1795 John Keats born at The Swan and Hoop | 1794 Blake, *Songs of Innocence and Songs of Experience*; Samuel Coleridge, *Monody on the Death of Chatterton* |
| 1796 Spain declares war on Britain | | |
| 1798 Suppression of Irish Rebellion | | 1798-1800 Wordsworth and Coleridge, *Lyrical Ballads* |
| 1800 Population of Great Britain and Ireland 9.5 million | 1802 Death of brother Edward; begins school in Enfield | 1802 *Edinburgh Review* founded |
| 1803 Renewed war with France | | 1803 Erasmus Darwin, *The Temple of Nature* |
| 1804 Napoleon crowned Emperor | 1804 Father thrown from horse and dies; mother remarries; children go to live with grandparents | |
| 1805 Battle of Trafalgar | 1805 Grandfather dies | 1805 Walter Scott, *The Lay of the Last Minstrel* |
| 1807 Abolition of slave trade in British possession | | 1807 Wordsworth, *Poems in Two volumes* |
| | 1810 Mother dies of TB | 1810 Birth of Tennyson |
| 1811 Prince of Wales becomes Regent; Luddite riots | 1811 John leaves school; apprenticed to surgeon | 1811 Jane Austen, *Sense and Sensibility* |
| 1812 Luddite riots spread; Elgin marbles arrive in London | | 1812 Byron, *Childe Harold's Pilgrimage*; birth of Robert Browning |
| 1813-17 Luddites hanged; Leigh Hunt imprisoned for attacking Prince Regent | | 1813 Percy Bysshe Shelley, *Queen Mab* |
| 1814 Allies invade France | 1814 Begins writing poetry; grandmother dies | 1814 Wordsworth, *The Excursion*; Scott, *Waverley* |

| Events in Europe | Author's life | Literary events |
| --- | --- | --- |
| **1815** Napoleon becomes Emperor again and is defeated; Corn Laws passed | **1815** Student at Guy's Hospital | |
| **1816** Riots after bad harvest and heavy taxation | **1816** Qualifies as apothecary; 'O Solitude' published | **1816** Coleridge, *Christabel*, *Kubla Khan* |
| **1817** Civil unrest continues | **1817** *Poems* | **1817** Coleridge, *Biographia Literaria* |
| | **1818** 'Isabella'; 'Hyperion: a Fragment'; brother George emigrates to America; brother Tom dies of TB; walking tour of N. England and Scotland; meets Fanny Brawne; *Endymion* published; *Blackwood's Magazine* attacks Keats and 'Cockney School' | **1818** Mary Shelley, *Frankenstein* |
| **1819** Peterloo Massacre in Manchester; repressive measures passed to prevent sedition; employment of children under nine in cotton mills forbidden; | **1819** Living in Hampstead; engaged to Fanny; TB active in autumn; writes 'Eve of St Agnes', 'Bright Star', 'Ode to Psyche', 'Ode to a Nightingale', 'Ode on a Grecian Urn', 'Ode on Melancholy', 'Fall of Hyperion', 'Lamia' | **1819** Byron, *Don Juan* |
| **1820** Death of George III and accession of George IV; plot to murder Cabinet fails | **1820** Feb.: severe haemorrhaging; Sept.: leaves for Italy; *Lamia, Isabella, Eve of St Agnes & Other Poems* published | **1820** John Clare, *Poems, Descriptive of Rural Life* |
| **1821** Greece revolts against Turks | **1821** February: dies in Rome | **1821** Shelley, *Adonais* (in memory of Keats) |

# FURTHER READING

## WORKS CITED

Walter Jackson Bate, ed. *Keats: A Collection of Critical Essays*, Prentice Hall, 1964

Andrew Bennett, *Keats, Narrative and Audience. The Posthumous Life of Writing*, Cambridge University Press, 1994

Alan J. Bewell, 'Keats's "Realm of Flora,"' *Studies in Romanticism*, 31, 1992, pp. 71–98
   Useful article on the gender implications of Keats's use of language

Cleanth Brooks, *The Well Wrought Urn*, 1947

G.H. Ford, *Keats and the Victorians*, Yale University Press, 1944

Margaret Homans, 'Keats Reading Women, Women Reading Keats,' *Studies in Romanticism*, 29, 1990, pp. 341–70

Paul de Man, ed., *The Selected Poetry of John Keats*, Signet, 1966

Jerome J. McGann, 'Keats and the Historical Method in Literary Criticism', *MLN*, 94, 1979, pp. 988–1032

Marjorie Levinson, *Keats's Life of Allegory: The Origins of a Style*, Blackwell, 1988

G.M. Matthews, ed., *Keats. The Critical Heritage*, Routledge, 1971
   A collection of the early criticism of Keats, 1816–63

Anne K. Mellor, *Romanticism and Gender*, Routledge, 1993

Nicholas Roe, *John Keats and the Culture of Dissent*, Clarendon, 1997

Hyder Edward Rollins, ed., *The Letters of John Keats*, Harvard University Press, 1958

Helen Vendler, *The Odes of John Keats*, Harvard University Press, 1983

Daniel P. Watkins, *Keats's Poetry and the Politics of the Imagination*, Toronto University Press, 1989

Susan Wolfson, 'Feminising Keats', in Hermione de Almeida, ed., *Critical Essays on John Keats*, G.K. Hall, 1990, pp. 317–56
   Demonstrates how the contemporary reviews and later criticism constructed a feminised Keats

**FURTHER READING**

Hermione de Almeida, ed., *Critical Essays on John Keats*, G.K. Hall, 1990
A useful collection of essays dating from 1965 onwards

Douglas Bush, *John Keats. His Life and Writings*, Collier, 1966
General study which focuses on the story of Keats's life, his development as a poet, and the themes of his main works

David S. Ferris, *Silent Urns: Romanticism, Hellenism, Modernity*, Stanford University Press, 2000
Keats's treatment of ancient Greek culture

Ian Jack, *Keats and the Mirror of Art*, Clarendon, 1967
Very useful specialised study of Keats's knowledge of the visual arts. Invaluable for its illustrations

Donald Keesey, *Contexts for Criticism*, Mayfield, 1994
Provides introductory essays on various theoretical approaches followed by essays demonstrating the practical application: Keats's 'Ode on A Grecian Urn' is one of the three texts used for essays of application

Andrew Motion, *Keats*, Faber, 1997
Usefully relates Keats's life to the intellectual and political life of the time

Michael O'Neill (ed.), *Keats: Bicentenary Readings*, Edinburgh University Press, 1997
Another collection of critical essays

Donald Reiman, ed., The *Romantics Reviewed: Contemporary Reviews of British Romantic Writers*, Garland, 1972
A useful collection of contemporary notices

Christopher Ricks, *Keats and Embarrassment*, Oxford University Press, 1976
Stimulating study which argues that through its aurally and visually embarrassing representations, the poetry induces in the reader a state of painful self-consciousness

Nicholas Roe, ed., *Keats and History*, Cambridge University Press, 1995
Provides an excellent example of the wide variety of contemporary historicist approaches to Keats's poetry, drawing upon the fields of politics, social history, feminism, economics, stylistics and aesthetics

# FURTHER READING

Robert M. Ryan and Ronald A. Sharp (eds), *The Persistence of Poetry: Bicentennial Essays on Keats*, University of Massachusetts Press, 1998
  Selection of critical essays demonstrating contemporary approaches

Grant E. Scott, 'Language Strange: A Visual History of Keats's "La Belle Dame sans Merci"', *Studies in Romanticism* 38.4, 1999, pp. 503–35
  Discusses visual representations of the poem

Stuart M. Sperry, *Keats the Poet*, Princeton University Press, 1973
  Particularly interesting on Keats's poetic processes

Jack Stillinger, *Reading the Eve of St Agnes: The Multiples of Complex Literary Transaction*, Oxford University Press, 1999
  Includes a listing of fifty-nine different interpretations of the poem, each with some supporting commentary. An Appendix presents a complete reading text of St Agnes, with apparatus

Brian Stone, *The Poetry of Keats*, Penguin, 1992
  A useful and accessible introductory study of the life and the work of Keats

Earl Wasserman, *The Finer Tone. Keats's Major Poems*, Johns Hopkins University Press, 1953
  Detailed textual analysis of the odes, 'La Belle Dame sans Merci', 'The Eve of St Agnes', and 'Lamia'

# LITERARY TERMS

**alexandrine** the most common metre in French poetry: a line of twelve syllables. The nearest English equivalent is the iambic hexameter; it is used as the last line in Spenserian stanzas; see 'The Eve of St Agnes'

**allegory** an allegorical story exists as an autonomous narrative, but has another hidden second meaning. *Endymion* has been seen as an allegory of the poet's quest for eternal truth and beauty

**anaphora** a rhetorical device in which a word or phrase is repeated in several successive clauses. See for example the repetition of questions beginning with 'what' in the opening stanza of 'Ode on a Grecian Urn'

**antithesis** opposing or contrasting ideas in neighbouring sentences or clauses, using opposite or strongly contrasting forms of words. When Keats's Isabella kisses the decomposing head of her lover, the narrator observes '…for the general award of love,/The little sweet doth kill much bitterness'

**apostrophe** rhetorical term for a speech addressed to a person, idea or thing, such as at the beginning of 'Ode on a Grecian Urn'

**art for art's sake** a movement in the arts flourishing during the second half of the nineteenth century which stressed the paramount value and self-sufficiency of art. Keats was considered a forerunner of this movement by many late nineteenth-century writers

**ballad** a poem or song which tells a story in simple, colloquial language

**blank verse** unrhymed iambic pentameter: a line of five iambs. One of the commonest of English metres. The two Hyperion poems are written in blank verse

**caesura** a pause within a line of verse. In this example from 'Ode on Melancholy', there are caesuras in both lines 'And Joy, whose hand is ever at his lips / Bidding adieu; and aching Pleasure nigh'

**canon** originally appropriated to describe the 'great works' of literature, it is now used to describe any group of books that becomes considered of value by a particular group of people at any given time

**closure** the impression of completeness and finality achieved by the ending of some literary works

**couplet** a pair of rhymed lines, of any metre. 'Bright Star' ends with the couplet 'Still, still to hear her tender-taken breath, / And so live ever – or else swoon to death'. A closed couplet makes grammatical sense by itself while a run-on couplet relies for its meaning on either the previous or the following line or both; heroic couplets lines of iambic pentameter rhymed in pairs. 'Lamia' is written in heroic couplets

**dialectic** the interplay of irreconcilable contradictory principles or opposed forces; this is usually now opposed to synthesis, but some versions of dialectical philosophy speak of a unification of opposites in which the thesis is opposed by the antithesis but united with it in a higher synthesis

**end-stopped** the end of a line of verse coincides with an essential grammatical pause usually signalled by punctuation: In the following example from 'Bright Star', the first line is end-stopped, the second enjambed: 'Bright star! would I were steadfast as thou art – / Not in lone splendour hung aloft the night / And watching …'

**elegy** an elaborately formal lyric poem lamenting the death of a single person

**enjambment** the running over of the sense and grammatical structure from one verse line or couplet to the next without a punctuated pause. Keats used this frequently in *Endymion*.

**feminist criticism** within feminist criticism there are numerous different positions. One of the main tenets of feminist thought is that male ways of perceiving and ordering are inscribed into the prevailing ideology of society and into language itself. Many feminist critics argue that patriarchal culture is marked by the urge to define, categorise, and control, and that it subjects thought to binary systems of irreconcilable opposites. Language is phallogocentric in that it privileges the male and subordinates the female, always associating the feminine with the less desirable term in the listed pairs; for example:

male/female
self/other
activity/passivity
culture/nature
day/night
head/heart
rational/irrational

Femininity is therefore considered a construction of society and of language. Sexual identity, what we are born with, becomes distinct from gender, which would include those traits we are encouraged to acquire and those traits which we are assigned by phallogocentric language. In Simone de Beauvoir's famous words from *The Second Sex*: 'One is not born, but rather becomes, a woman.' The same of course could be said of masculinity: it is a construct. The important difference is that in a patriarchal society, feminists would argue, men are in control of the definitions.

formalist criticism approach to literature in which form is emphasised as the chief criterion of value. Formalist critics generally avoid considerations external to the poem, such as biography or socio-historical context. The main tenet of formalist criticism is that the language of literature differs from ordinary language and the critic's task is to define this 'literariness'. For formalists, the quality of the language is more important than its denotative aspects. They are interested in close readings of the text with particular reference to form, style and technique. 'Practical criticism' is the name given to the formalist approach practised by the English critic F.R. Leavis and his followers in the first half of this century. The explication of texts or close reading was also practised by the American formalist school of New Criticism.

Recent theories about the instability of language have undermined the concern with the unity of the text, the rise of historicism has attacked its autonomy; and both feminist and post-colonial criticism have demonstrated the supposed 'universality' of great works to be no more than the workings of ideology.

heroic couplet see **couplet**

historicism the idea that all systems of thought must be seen within a historical perspective; traditional historicist critics attempt to place a literary work within its historical context

iambic pentameter an iambic foot has an unstressed followed by a stressed syllable; a pentameter has five feet; an iambic pentameter is therefore scanned as -/ -/ -/ -/ -/. An example from 'Isabella' is 'A thousand men in troubles wide and dark'

iconic the way in which a poem appears to be autonomous, as if it were an object to be contemplated, like a religious icon

imagery in its narrowest sense an image is a word-picture, a description of some visible scene or object. More commonly, 'imagery' refers to the figurative language, such as **metaphors** or **similes**, in a piece of literature, or to words which refer to objects and qualities which appeal to the senses and feelings. Keats uses imagery in every sense of its meaning

*in media res* (Lat. 'in the middle of things') a common technique of story-telling in which the narrator begins in the middle of the story. 'Hyperion' opens *'in media res'* with the Titans already deposed

lacuna a gap or break in the text

lyric a poem, usually short, expressing in a personal manner the feelings and thoughts of an individual speaker (not necessarily those of the poet). Keats's sonnets and odes are in the lyric form

Marxist criticism criticism which considers literature in relation to its capacity to reflect the struggle between the classes, and the economic conditions which, according to Karl Marx and Friedrich Engels, lie at the basis of man's intellectual and social evolution. A Marxist critic would be particularly interested in Keats's attack on the capitalist brothers in 'Isabella'

metaphor goes further than a comparison between two different things or ideas, by fusing them together. Keats's metaphors are generally implicit rather than explicit, and often fuse even more than two things together. In the opening line of 'On first looking into Chapman's Homer', for example, 'realms of gold' conflates poetry with the Greek islands and with the New World

metonym a figure of speech in which an idea is evoked by means of a term of some associated notion, such as Grub Street for hack writers

New Criticism a major critical movement of the 1930s and 1940s in the US. The new critics argued for the autonomy of literature, studied in isolation from its biographical and historical context. They saw the work as a linguistic structure in which all the parts are held together as an organic whole; their emphasis was on form and structure

new historicist criticism this school of criticism, which developed mainly in the area of Romantic and Shakespearean studies, contextualises the literary work, focusing particularly on the production, transmission and reception of the text in literary history

octave a stanza of eight lines, or the first eight lines of a sonnet

ode a lyric poem, characterised by its length, intricate stanza forms, grandeur of style and seriousness of purpose. The form was established by the Greek poet Pindar. Many English poets have experimented with variations of the ode

ottava rima an eight-line iambic stanza, rhyming abababcc. 'Isabella' in written in ottava rima

oxymoron a figure of speech in which contradictory terms are brought together in what is at first sight an impossible combination: a special variety of paradox

paradox an apparently self-contradictory statement which nevertheless holds some meaning or truth. Keats's urn is silent, for example but it is also a historian who tells sylvan tales

parallelism the building up of a sentence or statement using repeated syntactic units. Parallelism achieves an effect of balance. It is used, for example, in stanza 3 of 'Ode to a Nightingale'

personification a variety of figurative or metaphorical language in which things or ideas are treated as if they were human beings. Keats personifies such abstract qualities as joy and beauty in 'Ode on Melancholy'

Post-Structuralist building on work begun by Saussure in the field of linguistics, in Post-Structuralism meaning is not inherent in words, but depends on their mutual relationships within the system of language, a system defined on difference

psychoanalytical criticism Freud developed the theory of psychoanalysis as a means of curing neuroses in his patients; its concepts have been expanded as a means of understanding human behaviour and culture generally

register literary critics sometimes use register to denote a kind of language being used, especially the kind of language appropriate to a particular situation

Romanticism see **Literary background**

Romantic irony an eighteenth- and nineteenth-century German term for the kind of narrative in which the author constantly breaks the illusion being created. Keats's digressions in 'Isabella' and 'The Eve of St Agnes', for example, constantly draw our attention to the fact that these are just stories

self-conscious narrator self-conscious narrators constantly draw attention to the fact they are creating a work of art for the purpose of exploring the conventions under which they are operating. Keats's digressions on romance in 'Isabella' provide one example

sestet a stanza of six lines, or the last six lines of a **Petrarchan sonnet**

simile a figure of speech in which one thing is said to be like another and the comparison is made with the use of 'like' or 'as'. epic simile a long simile, sometimes over twenty lines, which typically interrupts the narrative in an epic poem, allowing the poet to make detailed comparisons. Keats uses these primarily in *Hyperion*

sonnet a lyric poem of fourteen lines of iambic pentameter rhymed and organised according to several intricate schemes. The Italian poet Petrarch established the sonnet as a major poetic form in his *Canzoniere* (c. 1335). Petrarchan or Italian sonnets are divided into a set of eight lines, or octave, and a set of six lines, or sestet, rhymed *abbaabba cde cde* (or *cdcdcd*) Shakespearean sonnets are divided into three sets of four lines, or quatrains, and a couplet, rhymed *abab bcbc cdcd ee*

Spenserian stanza a form invented by Edmund Spenser for *The Faerie Queene* (1590, 1596). Eight lines of iambic pentameter followed by an alexandrine, rhyming *ababbcbcc*. 'The Eve of St Agnes' is in Spenserian stanzas

spondee a metrical foot consisting of two long syllables or two strong stresses

synaesthesia the description of a sense impression in terms more appropriate to a different sense; the mixing of sense impressions. Keats makes particularly effective use of this in stanza 2 of 'Ode to a Nightingale'

transcendent that which is 'above' and independent of the material universe; knowledge beyond the limits of human experience

trimeter a line consisting of three feet. Examples can be found in 'La Belle Dame sans Merci'

valediction a farewell speech. 'To Autumn' is in the valedictory mode

volta the change in mood and argument which occurs between the octave and sestet of a sonnet

Glennis Byron is Reader in English Studies at the University of Stirling. She is the author of *Letitia Landon. The Woman Behind L.E.L.*, Manchester, 1995, and the editor of *Dracula. The Casebook*, Macmillan, 1998, *Dracula*, Broadview, 1997, and *Nineteenth-Century Stories by Women*, Broadview, 1995.

*General editors*

Martin Gray, former Head of the Department of English Studies at the University of Stirling, and of Literary Studies at the University of Luton

Professor A. N. Jeffares, Emeritus Professor of English, University of Stirling

Maya Angelou
*I Know Why the Caged Bird Sings*

Jane Austen
*Pride and Prejudice*

Alan Ayckbourn
*Absent Friends*

Elizabeth Barrett Browning
*Selected Poems*

Robert Bolt
*A Man for All Seasons*

Harold Brighouse
*Hobson's Choice*

Charlotte Brontë
*Jane Eyre*

Emily Brontë
*Wuthering Heights*

Shelagh Delaney
*A Taste of Honey*

Charles Dickens
*David Copperfield*
*Great Expectations*
*Hard Times*
*Oliver Twist*

Roddy Doyle
*Paddy Clarke Ha Ha Ha*

George Eliot
*Silas Marner*
*The Mill on the Floss*

Anne Frank
*The Diary of a Young Girl*

William Golding
*Lord of the Flies*

Oliver Goldsmith
*She Stoops to Conquer*

Willis Hall
*The Long and the Short and the Tall*

Thomas Hardy
*Far from the Madding Crowd*
*The Mayor of Casterbridge*
*Tess of the d'Urbervilles*
*The Withered Arm and other Wessex Tales*

L.P. Hartley
*The Go-Between*

Seamus Heaney
*Selected Poems*

Susan Hill
*I'm the King of the Castle*

Barry Hines
*A Kestrel for a Knave*

Louise Lawrence
*Children of the Dust*

Harper Lee
*To Kill a Mockingbird*

Laurie Lee
*Cider with Rosie*

Arthur Miller
*The Crucible*
*A View from the Bridge*

Robert O'Brien
*Z for Zachariah*

Frank O'Connor
*My Oedipus Complex and Other Stories*

George Orwell
*Animal Farm*

J.B. Priestley
*An Inspector Calls*
*When We Are Married*

Willy Russell
*Educating Rita*
*Our Day Out*

J.D. Salinger
*The Catcher in the Rye*

William Shakespeare
*Henry IV Part I*
*Henry V*
*Julius Caesar*
*Macbeth*
*The Merchant of Venice*
*A Midsummer Night's Dream*
*Much Ado About Nothing*
*Romeo and Juliet*
*The Tempest*
*Twelfth Night*

George Bernard Shaw
*Pygmalion*

Mary Shelley
*Frankenstein*

R.C. Sherriff
*Journey's End*

Rukshana Smith
*Salt on the snow*

John Steinbeck
*Of Mice and Men*

Robert Louis Stevenson
*Dr Jekyll and Mr Hyde*

Jonathan Swift
*Gulliver's Travels*

Robert Swindells
*Daz 4 Zoe*

Mildred D. Taylor
*Roll of Thunder, Hear My Cry*

Mark Twain
*Huckleberry Finn*

James Watson
*Talking in Whispers*

Edith Wharton
*Ethan Frome*

William Wordsworth
*Selected Poems*

*A Choice of Poets*

*Mystery Stories of the Nineteenth Century including The Signalman*

*Nineteenth Century Short Stories*

*Poetry of the First World War*

*Six Women Poets*

**For the AQA Anthology:**

*Duffy and Armitage & Pre-1914 Poetry*

*Heaney and Clarke & Pre-1914 Poetry*

*Poems from Different Cultures*

Margaret Atwood
*Cat's Eye*
*The Handmaid's Tale*

Jane Austen
*Emma*
*Mansfield Park*
*Persuasion*
*Pride and Prejudice*
*Sense and Sensibility*

Alan Bennett
*Talking Heads*

William Blake
*Songs of Innocence and of
Experience*

Charlotte Brontë
*Jane Eyre*
*Villette*

Emily Brontë
*Wuthering Heights*

Angela Carter
*Nights at the Circus*

Geoffrey Chaucer
*The Franklin's Prologue and Tale*
*The Merchant's Prologue and
Tale*
*The Miller's Prologue and Tale*
*The Prologue to the Canterbury
Tales*
*The Wife of Bath's Prologue and
Tale*

Samuel Coleridge
*Selected Poems*

Joseph Conrad
*Heart of Darkness*

Daniel Defoe
*Moll Flanders*

Charles Dickens
*Bleak House*
*Great Expectations*
*Hard Times*

Emily Dickinson
*Selected Poems*

John Donne
*Selected Poems*

Carol Ann Duffy
*Selected Poems*

George Eliot
*Middlemarch*
*The Mill on the Floss*

T.S. Eliot
*Selected Poems*
*The Waste Land*

F. Scott Fitzgerald
*The Great Gatsby*

E.M. Forster
*A Passage to India*

Brian Friel
*Translations*

Thomas Hardy
*Jude the Obscure*
*The Mayor of Casterbridge*
*The Return of the Native*
*Selected Poems*
*Tess of the d'Urbervilles*

Seamus Heaney
*Selected Poems from 'Opened
Ground'*

Nathaniel Hawthorne
*The Scarlet Letter*

Homer
*The Iliad*
*The Odyssey*

Aldous Huxley
*Brave New World*

Kazuo Ishiguro
*The Remains of the Day*

Ben Jonson
*The Alchemist*

James Joyce
*Dubliners*

John Keats
*Selected Poems*

Philip Larkin
*The Whitsun Weddings and
Selected Poems*

Christopher Marlowe
*Doctor Faustus*
*Edward II*

Arthur Miller
*Death of a Salesman*

John Milton
*Paradise Lost Books I & II*

Toni Morrison
*Beloved*

George Orwell
*Nineteen Eighty-Four*

Sylvia Plath
*Selected Poems*

Alexander Pope
*Rape of the Lock & Selected
Poems*

William Shakespeare
*Antony and Cleopatra*
*As You Like It*
*Hamlet*
*Henry IV Part I*
*King Lear*
*Macbeth*
*Measure for Measure*
*The Merchant of Venice*
*A Midsummer Night's Dream*
*Much Ado About Nothing*
*Othello*
*Richard II*
*Richard III*
*Romeo and Juliet*
*The Taming of the Shrew*
*The Tempest*
*Twelfth Night*
*The Winter's Tale*

George Bernard Shaw
*Saint Joan*

Mary Shelley
*Frankenstein*

Jonathan Swift
*Gulliver's Travels and A Modest
Proposal*

Alfred Tennyson
*Selected Poems*

Virgil
*The Aeneid*

Alice Walker
*The Color Purple*

Oscar Wilde
*The Importance of Being
Earnest*

Tennessee Williams
*A Streetcar Named Desire*
*The Glass Menagerie*

Jeanette Winterson
*Oranges Are Not the Only Fruit*

John Webster
*The Duchess of Malfi*

Virginia Woolf
*To the Lighthouse*

William Wordsworth
*The Prelude and Selected Poems*

W.B. Yeats
*Selected Poems*

*Metaphysical Poets*

# The diary of
# A WORLD WAR II
# PILOT

by Dennis Hamley
Illustrated by Brian Duggan

# W
# FRANKLIN WATTS
LONDON•SYDNEY

# 7 September 1938

My name is Johnny Hedley. I live in a small town in the Midlands with my parents. My father is Headmaster of a junior school. I have one younger sister, Janet. I went to the local grammar school and then started work in a bank. Boring. But yesterday was my eighteenth birthday and today I start my diary of life in the Royal Air Force, the RAF. Well, I'm not actually in it yet, but I soon will be. I'm going to join up. Not the real RAF yet but the RAF Volunteer Reserve to learn to fly. I think it's the least I can do.

There'll be a war. Everybody knows it except, it seems, Mr Chamberlain, the Prime Minister. "Peace for our time," he said, when he came back from Munich with that bit of paper signed by Nazi leader Adolf Hitler. I reckon that if Chamberlain believes that, he'll believe anything. Can't he see that Hitler is a rat?

They say the next war will be fought in the air. I want to fly fighters. It's better than working in a bank any day.

I feel so excited I won't sleep tonight.

# 8 SEPTEMBER 1938

Back again. What a let-down. I queued up outside the RAF Volunteer Reserve Centre in Coventry with about fifty others. They were a mixed bunch. I met a lord and an unemployed welder. But when I reached the front of the queue, the recruiting officer told me to come back in two months. A lot of us met up again outside and we've all been told the same thing, even the lord. So we went to the nearest pub instead.

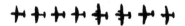

I reckon I might make some good mates in this bunch. The lord's name is David Albury. Lord David Albury really, but he doesn't like the "lord" bit. He'll be a duke when his dad dies. "But with this war coming I'll probably go," he said. He's tall and thin, with dark hair. The welder's name is Jim Bassett. He's short, but he looks strong. I come in the middle, but I've got fair hair. We're friends already. "Through thick and thin," said Jim.

# 5 NOVEMBER 1938

Good news at last. We're to report to an Initial Flying Training School in Norfolk, for the first steps in flying real aeroplanes.

# 9 November 1938

We got here in darkness, after hours on a very slow train. It wheezed into a tiny station and we scrambled off, to be met by RAF corporals screaming at us to get in line, and marched down a dark lane to the Training Wing, where they shoved us into old wooden huts. Our hut is lined with ten small beds either side and a coal stove at one end. Beside each bed is a locker and a wardrobe. David, Jim and I are sticking together already.

So this is it. A miserable dump. Not what we expected.

# 10 November 1938

This is more like it. We were woken up at 6.30, had a putrid breakfast in the airmen's mess and then reported to the equipment store. They issued us with flying suits and helmets with strange pipes hanging from them. These are Gosport tubes, speaking tubes so the instructors can talk to us over the noise of the plane's engine.

Then we waited to be assessed by the instructors. We went in one by one alphabetically, so David and Jim saw them before me. David came out looking pale. He sat down heavily and muttered, "Don't let them intimidate you." Jim was fourth in. He came out, red-faced with anger and said, very audibly, "They're b–."

"No swearing," the sergeant roared before Jim could finish, but I got the point all right.

My turn came. I felt really scared as I entered

the room. In front of me, behind a long table, sat twelve RAF officers, some with moustaches, all looking very fierce. I sat down on a small wooden chair. They glared at me and I felt like the little boy in that painting called *When did you last see your father?* They started grilling me: "Why do you want to join up? What makes you think you can fly a fighter? Could you take off knowing you probably won't come back?" At the end I felt a miserable worm with no right to join the RAF. When they let me go, I staggered out and sat down between David and Jim. "I think I'll be going home today," I whispered. "I'll be on the train with you," Jim answered.

The interviews lasted till early afternoon. We were marched off for something to eat, then back to hear our fates. An instructor came out and pinned a sheet of paper on the wall.

We swarmed round it – and cheered. We've all got teachers. That means we're not going home.

My instructor is Flying Officer Parker. He's very sunburnt. He's just come back from the Middle East, where he flew Hawker Furies on border patrols. "One day you'll fly these wonderful new Spitfires and Hurricanes," he said. "They make even the Fury look like something out of the last war."

But now we have to start on little Tiger Moths, biplanes with two cockpits, so the pupil sits in front and the instructor behind. Really easy to fly. So they say!

I was looking forward so much to getting off the ground, but it didn't happen yet. "First thing," said Flying Officer Parker, "is knowing how to start this thing. You won't always have a mechanic to do it for you."

What you have to do is to make sure everything is switched off, go through the drill with the switches, get out, grab the propeller and swing it hard. This makes the engine spark. Then you get out of the way quick, unless you want your head taken off. That's happened a few times, he says. Then you jump in the cockpit quick, or the plane will roll away without you.

Oh, the hurdles we jump before we can fly! I was scared as I took hold of the prop, but I gave it a swing, leapt out of the way, heard the engine roar and scrambled into the cockpit. But then he made me do it again and again. It didn't get less scary. When will they find a better way to start aeroplanes up?

This evening, us mates talked about our experiences. Jim and David had started up without mishap – and no one had his head cut off. But one bloke lost two fingers. We won't see him again. This flying lark is dangerous, even before you get airborne. It hasn't put me off, though. I still want more than anything to be up there in the sky.

# 9 NOVEMBER 1938

Ah, but today was magical. We were up at 6.30 again, on a clear, cold day. The Tiger Moths were waiting as we trudged towards them in our flying suits and helmets. Flying Officer Parker gave me instructions all the way. "Put your hand round the stick and your feet on the rudder bar, but don't, for God's sake, try to work the controls. Remember, they're duplicated. Just feel how I operate them in the cockpit behind you. Listen to what I say and remember what I do."

At least we didn't have to push the propeller ourselves. A ground mechanic was waiting. He saluted Flying Officer Parker and winked at me. I climbed into the front cockpit, strapped myself in, put my goggles on and waited. I heard Flying Officer Parker behind me, calling to the mechanic: "Petrol on. Switches off. Suck in," (meaning "get petrol into the carburetor"), as the mechanic heaved on the propeller. Then: "Ready to start. Petrol on. Switches on. Contact!"

The engine's roar was deafening. I saw the

mechanic jump out of the way as we taxied slowly forward over the rough grass, then bump, bump, bump, faster and faster until we seemed dangerously near the hedge at the edge of the airfield, then a feeling of lightness as the little Tiger Moth stopped being a clumsy mass of metal, wire and canvas and became a live thing, free in the air and climbing, climbing. I will never forget that moment, seeing the ground below us and our huts, the windsock and the camp Headquarters tiny like toys. I knew I was in my element, the place where I'm meant to be. I'm just eighteen, and master of the skies!

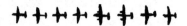

Then I realised I was heaving back on the joystick and F/O Parker was shouting through the Gosport tube. "Let go, you idiot, or you'll stall us."

I let go quickly and felt him take the little plane straight and level. He banked to the left and the right, then suddenly flew upside-down, which turned my stomach upside-down with it. He righted us and then climbed so steeply that we lost all our speed, the engine cut out and we fell like a stone. I was terrified! But then I felt the stick in my hands push forwards, we dived, the engine restarted and we flew straight and level again.

"That," said Flying Officer Parker through the Gosport tube, "is a stall. If you know what you're doing, you can get out of it." He then added, "Usually." He let me take the controls and I made the plane go all over the place. I couldn't co-ordinate my hand on the joystick with my feet on the rudder bars. After about ten minutes, I realised this flying caper wasn't as easy as I thought! Then Flying Officer Parker said: "Give her back to me. We'll loop the loop and go home."

Looping the loop. Oh my God. Without warning, he put us in a steep dive. Terrifying. People in their gardens below looked up at us. I could see their faces, they were that close. "We'll smash your runner beans," I thought in a panic. Then he pulled sharply out of the dive and climbed again. I was rammed into the back of my seat. But instead of pulling out he kept going up, so we were upside-down again. Then he dived again. I thought my insides were coming out. But he kept going, making a huge circle until we were flying straight and level again.

My heart was thudding and there was a roaring in my ears. When it died down, F/O Parker was talking. "Wasn't that wonderful?" That's not the word I would have used!

We headed home. "Landing," said F/O Parker. "The most difficult thing of all. Some people never learn. Of course, they might have in the end if they hadn't killed themselves first."

He's got a strange sense of humour, I thought as I watched his steady approach, wingtips dead level with the horizon, a slow, shallow descent and then the slightest bump as he made a perfect landing. He taxied to a halt, we got out, took our helmets off and looked back at the Tiger Moth. My legs were wobbling like jelly.

He clapped me cheerfully on the back. "Piece of cake, that little crate," he said. "Soon you'll fly planes four times as fast and ten times as powerful." But I didn't feel like master of the skies as I staggered into the hut. More like the office junior!

## 12 JANUARY 1939

So it's goodbye to my first training school, the
Tiger Moths and Flying Officer Parker and home
for some leave. I can fly solo, get out of a spin
(just about), land with my engine cut out, fly by
instruments with the cockpit hooded, do simple
navigation and a bit of aerobatics. I've had yards
of theory dinned into me, though I've forgotten
half already. Oh, and though I haven't got a
uniform yet, I'm an Acting Pilot Officer. So is
David. Jim isn't, and I think that's rotten. He'll be
a sergeant-pilot, a non-commissioned officer,
while we have the King's Commission and live in
the Officers' Mess. I reckon it's because David's
an aristocrat and at least I'm a bank clerk but he's
only a welder. That's the RAF for you.

## 15 MARCH 1939

Yesterday I came to the Advanced Training
School at RAF Leuchars in Scotland. I left home
at six in the morning and got here at nearly
midnight. David was the first person I met.

Jim's going somewhere else. After a shivering night in a tin Nissen hut on which falling rain sounded like hailstones, we signed in at the Guard Room early this morning and then reported to the Officers' Mess, where Wing-Commanders and Group Captains looked at us as though we were dirt.

Why haven't I written anything for two months? Because I've been too worn out. Before coming here, David and I were at an RAF camp quite near home. We never went near an aeroplane but had days of marching and arms drill on the parade ground, being screamed at by drill-instructor corporals and sergeants, route marches and being told how we should behave as officers (not talking about politics, religion or women at dinner in the Mess – silly, I never talk about politics or religion). We were also told what happens if we break the rules (from being confined to camp, to kicked out of the Service) and how to salute. And, more importantly, who to salute. There was endless cleaning and polishing. But everyone has to put up with it before the real life starts. At last, a uniform came, specially made for me. It cost £80 (the RAF paid). Once mine was on I felt I really belonged.

## 16 MARCH 1939

There are two sorts of aircraft here. First are Hawker Harts, biplanes which were front-line fighters a few years ago, but which the Germans would eat for breakfast today. They put us on

14

those first, to make sure we still knew what we were doing. It was amazing how quickly it all came back, though the instructors aren't so friendly, which makes us realise things are getting serious.

The Hart is bigger and more powerful than the dear old Tiger Moth, but in the end, one plane flies much like another. At least, that's how it seems. But there's a line of stubby-looking monoplanes in a different part of the airfield. American Harvards. Our advanced trainers – and a lot nearer to what we'll soon be flying in action.

✝ ✝ ✝ ✝ ✝ ✝ ✝ ✝

## 27 AUGUST 1939

My first real posting. I'm at Biggin Hill, in Kent, on top of the North Downs, where the runway ends on the edge of the hill. I've joined a Hurricane squadron now I've been trained on this wonderful plane.

It's sleek, low and streamlined, has eight machine guns and does 320 miles an hour. Wow! The moment I sat in the cockpit, I thought the plane was perfection. When I took it in the air, got used to it quickly, threw it round the sky a little, I knew it was. Now I'm a real flier of fighters, Pilot Officer Hedley, with my pilot's wings sewn on to my uniform.

So I'm ready for war. The trouble is, there isn't one – yet. But Hitler has invaded Poland

and Czechoslovakia and he's keen to get at France. Whether Mr Chamberlain likes it or not, war will come soon enough. We're thankful now that Chamberlain brought that bit of paper back from Munich. We have had a year to get ready. Better than nothing. Still, when I look at the squadron lined up, it doesn't seem that big. We hear about whole legions of aircraft from the Luftwaffe – the German Air Force – ready to oppose us.

I've made a good friend here. His name is Dai and he comes from near Cardiff. He's big and burly and he's brilliant at rugby.

## 3 SEPTEMBER 1939

It's begun. Mr Chamberlain told us on the radio. "Britain is in a state of war against Germany." So the waiting is over. At first I was glad. Then, though I won't tell anyone else, I felt frightened. War's here and I have to fight it when I could have stayed safe at home. A few minutes later, air-raid sirens blared and we took off. To and fro we flew, looking for the hordes of German bombers. Nothing. An empty sky. Big let-down.

## 7 SEPTEMBER 1939

We hear that four Hurricane squadrons are off to France, to help the army. I wish we were one of them. Meanwhile we do patrols over the sea day after day to stop Germans bombing our shipping.

A few Jerry (German) planes have been shot down but we've never seen one.

## 20 NOVEMBER 1939

Hurrah! Our first "kill" today. We were over the Channel, off Dover, and we spotted a German Dornier over to get aerial photographs. Well, he won't show Hitler his snaps now. I think Sergeant Brown got him – he's been flying longer than the rest of us. He reminds me of Jim Bassett. Where have he and David been posted? I'd love to meet them again – my first Air Force friends.

# 31 DECEMBER 1939

Christmas has come and gone. I had a bit of leave, so I went home. All so familiar, yet it seemed another world. You wouldn't think there was a war on. They asked me lots of questions, but somehow I couldn't tell them anything. Dad could take it all right because he fought in the last war, but I'd worry about Mum.

I'm back now. Tonight we'll celebrate New Year in the local pubs. We might even chat up a nurse or two from the hospital. The weather's foul. We haven't flown for a month, either us or the Germans. I wish I was in France, fighting already to help the army. Surely 1940 will see the end of this "phoney war"?

## 15 MARCH 1940

I'm picking up the diary again. I'm still at Biggin Hill on endless patrols without an enemy plane in sight. We play cards while we're waiting. I play Dai for cigarettes. I've got good at cards and he's hopeless, so all I win is a nasty cough!

## 11 MAY 1940

Now the balloon really has gone up. Yesterday, the German army invaded France. Nobody expected it. They sent tanks round the Maginot Line, which we and the French thought would defend us for ever. They've cut the French army off. Will our soldiers beat them back? What about our fighter pilots? They've got the whole of the Luftwaffe to fight.

## 25 MAY 1940

Tomorrow, our war really starts. Operation Dynamo. Our armies are beaten, the Nazis are in Paris and occupy most of France. The British

Army is coming home. It won't be easy. We've heard pleas on the wireless for everyone who has a boat by the seaside to take it over the Channel to Dunkirk and get the soldiers off the French beaches. We must stop the German pilots bombing them.

Everybody was quiet tonight. Tomorrow could be a disaster.

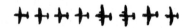

## 26 MAY 1940

How perfect the weather is. Dad's often told me of days in the last war, when birds sang and the sun shone as they went into action. We should be sunbathing, not taking off and perhaps never returning. I can't help feeling scared.

It's such a big day that I've got to write down the names of some of the friends besides Dai who'll be flying with me. The Squadron Commander is Squadron-Leader Neil MacLeish – a Scot from Edinburgh. He's a friend as well as the boss: we respect him – he'll never let us down. He's been in the RAF for ten years, flying all sorts of planes. There are two new Pilot-Officers like me, lowest of the low. Fred Summers and Peter Wilson. Then there's Sergeant Brown – a real tough nut. I don't want to tread on his toes. And so many others – all good blokes, but will we still have courage when the shooting starts? I lay awake last night wondering.

# 28 May 1940

We're back. It was a beautiful day as we crossed the Channel and came over France. But we were out of range of our Radio Direction Finding stations, so we were on our own.

I shall never forget what I saw today. As we crossed the beach at Dunkirk, I saw long lines of British soldiers, waiting patiently, queueing across the sand and far into the sea as the little ships came in as near as they dared to pick them up and take them back home. Beyond were Navy ships keeping them safe – I hope. We flew in low Most soldiers had no weapons. Where were their tanks and lorries? Had they destroyed them to stop the Germans getting them?

The Luftwaffe aren't far away. We had to cut them off so they couldn't shoot up the men. Because they would, don't you worry!

We climbed towards the sun and soon found them. A line of the dreaded German Stuka dive-bombers, flying below us, making for those lines of defenceless soldiers. Hadn't they seen us above them? Now my stomach really turned over. I'd only ever fought Germans in slow Dorniers and Heinkels and, though we've had a few mock battles with other RAF squadrons, I'd never met pilots flying the Stuka before.

We followed Neil MacLeish, keeping to the strict formation we'd been taught. He dived and we followed – out of the sun to surprise the enemy. I picked out one Stuka, got him in my gunsights and gave him a burst of fire. I think

I got him. At any rate, he disappeared. I looked round. We must have been having a field day. There were only six Stukas left. I saw Dai get another and the rest turned tail and made for home. We couldn't chase them – not enough fuel. I heard Neil on the intercom. "Make for home, quick as you can."

I turned. But suddenly I felt something rip through the Hurricane's body. Cannon shells. We must have been jumped out of the sun ourselves. Though I now seemed alone in the sky, I knew who'd nearly got me. It was my first meeting with a Messerschmitt 109, the main German fighter. Suddenly the sky was full of them. I saw a Hurricane spin into the sea, smoke pouring out of it. Dai. I knew the identification letters. He didn't bail out. He must be dead.

I couldn't stop to grieve. Now I saw what war in the air really meant.

All right, we turned and gave as good as we got. Jim shot down a Messerschmitt – I saw it clearly. The last I saw of Sergeant Brown was him chasing another with smoke pouring out of his engine. I wanted to scream, "Watch your tail!" as a Messerschmitt came up behind him. Sergeant Brown didn't stand a chance. Another Hurricane in the sea: another good man gone. I heard Neil on the intercom again. "For God's sake get back home!"

So I did, fast as I could. I reckoned it was best to live to fight another day though I knew my plane had been shot full of holes. I crossed the Channel OK and those old white cliffs were the greatest sight I've ever seen. But I soon knew I wouldn't make it all the way to Biggin Hill. I was low on fuel. The controls didn't respond properly. The Jerry in the Messerschmitt must have hit me worse than I thought. I was losing height. I thought I'd make for Lympne Airfield. But soon I knew I wouldn't make it. Best look for a farmer's field instead.

I saw one and lined myself up for a landing. But I couldn't get the wheels down. I'd have to belly-land. At least I might save bits of the Hurricane to be used as spares, if it didn't catch fire first with me in it. Watching the grass rush up towards me was torture. I tried to keep the wing-tips level with the horizon and pull the stick back to level out, but nothing seemed to work. There was a jarring, rending crash as we hit the ground. I must have lost consciousness for a moment, because when I'd undone the straps and struggled out, the Hurricane was surrounded by soldiers, air raid wardens and the farmer who owned the field, who didn't seem best pleased.

I was at Biggin Hill that evening. The Medical Officer gave me a quick check-up and then sent me back to the squadron. But it wasn't a happy homecoming. The squadron had flown three sorties altogether that day. Besides Dai and Sergeant Brown we'd lost two other pilots and five planes. Between us we'd shot down about eight Stukas and three Me 109s – but it didn't make up for the loss of good mates. Dai was my first real friend to be killed. He probably won't be the last. Still, this is what we joined for.

## 20 JUNE 1940

I've been so tired these last three weeks that I've had no inclination to write this diary, or do anything except the reports to make after the end of each mission. The campaign over France is over. The British Army, or as much of it as could be saved, is home. We've lost good people from the squadron. Peter Wilson baled out over France: we hope he's a prisoner of the Germans. Three days later we lost our squadron commander, Neil MacLeish, shot down over the Channel. But we kept the Luftwaffe away from the British soldiers and that was all that mattered.

Now it's very quiet. Replacement flyers arrive every day. New planes are delivered. We expect the Germans are doing the same: they got a mauling as well. Hitler says he'll invade us. A huge army is getting ready on the French coast. Our army is in no state to beat them back.

Goering, head of the Luftwaffe, boasts how he'll destroy British air power, and make us defenceless. We all know there'll be the mother and father of all air battles soon and if we don't win it, Britain is finished. It's enough to make you stay awake all night.

## 23 JUNE 1940

Great news! More replacements today. And one of them is David Albury. Wonderful. Together again. He's been stationed in the north of England, but he wanted to come where the action is! So here he is, with his little red MG two-seater sports car.

Some of us in the squadron go to the local pub, The Dog and Partridge, most nights while there's a lull. Each Saturday night there's a dance in the village and we often go there as well. It's a poky little hall with a scratchy band. They don't sound much like Joe Loss and his dance band, but they remind us of better times and we can meet some of the local talent. I'll lure David there next Saturday, with tales of a marvellous night life in store for him. I hope the reality won't disappoint him too much!

# 27 June 1940

Well, we all went to the dance. David took me in his MG. I came home feeling discontented. David and I stuck together and we met two girls, who were also sticking together. Shirley was lovely – a brunette. You could see that she liked David at once and he liked her. I was left with her friend Deanna. She was nice enough and looked great, but she never stopped talking! After two minutes my head ached. After a foxtrot and a quickstep to the slightly out-of-tune music of The Sharps and Flats, I could see that David and Shirley were not going to be separated and Deanna wouldn't lose sight of Shirley. So I had to stick with her so she wouldn't spoil things for David.

Difficult. She was getting on my nerves
as much as the squawky saxophone in the band.

I walked Deanna home – Shirley was in the
MG! I got back to the station on my own: David
didn't turn up until nearly two in the morning.
"You think you've clicked, don't you?" I said,
slightly irritated. "Reckon so," he answered and
went straight to sleep, a blissful smile on his face.

In the middle of the night I woke up thinking
how daft all this was. Shirley and David? Deanne
and me? Probably neither of us would be still
alive by Christmas.

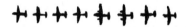

# 9 JULY 1940

The lull is over. Those boffins with their Radio
Direction Finding keep finding German planes
over the Channel and we go up to beat them off.
The Germans want to find out all about us.
To start the invasion. So we've got to stop them.

But until now they came alone, so they were
sitting ducks. Now these planes often have
Messerschmitt escorts. We're losing planes. Our
squadron was up four times today. David made
his first kill, a Dornier on reconnaissance, but
then a Messerschmitt shot him up and he limped
home with no fuel and a big hole in his fuselage.
The ground crew found a bullet hole in his fuel
tank. Thank God he got back. He was lucky.

# 12 JULY 1940

It's hotting up – the fighting, that is, not the weather, which is wet, miserable and with cloud you can hardly see through. The Germans are concentrating on the sea, bombing shipping, especially the coal convoys. You can see what their game is. If they draw us out over the sea they can pick us off and send half our planes to the bottom of the Channel. If we stay put, our ships will have no protection. This is serious. I hate the sea. The Germans carry rubber dinghies and have air-sea rescue boats to pick them up. We don't. Why not? If we land on the sea we'll sink. If we parachute into it, we'll probably drown. It doesn't make you feel good as you take off.

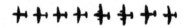

We flew four times today, starting at 6 a.m. We met the enemy once. As we flew over Beachy Head looking for a group of bombers we'd been told about, we were suddenly bounced by fifteen Messerschmitts coming on us from above. This was a shock. How had they got here without being spotted? It was every man for himself now. This Messerschmitt is a terrific plane. I hate to say it, but I reckon it's better than the Hurricane. I saw a couple of ours go down before I even got a sight of one of theirs. I gave it a quick burst before it disappeared. I didn't see it go down. But I thought that if I claimed it I might feel better.

We came back minus three Hurricanes. When we debriefed, we made our claims. I claimed my Messerschmitt 109, David claimed one: by the time we'd finished claiming it seemed we'd shot down nine Jerries. But I was worried. I reckon a lot more than six Germans went home safely.

## 4 AUGUST 1940

I must write something today or lose my diary habit. We're so tired. Constant flying, slicing through bombers, dogfighting with Messerschmitts, thinking you're a goner every minute, hardly any sleep; it's a wonder we can stand, let alone put fighters in the air every morning. There aren't many left who I joined the squadron with. David's survived – and he sees Shirley most nights. I don't know how he keeps going. Perhaps Shirley's the reason.

There have been new arrivals, a couple of Canadians, a South African and an Australian. There's also a Pole, Sergeant Dorosz. He fought through the German invasion of Poland, escaped, flew with the French Air Force, then managed to get here. He has a score to settle with the Germans. He speaks English perfectly well on the ground. In the air, he doesn't understand a word! It's hopeless getting him to keep to squadron tactics, so we let him do what he wants, flying all over the place and shooting at every Messerschmitt he sees. It seems to work. He's shot down six and he's a happy man.

When I read today's diary entry I felt uncomfortable. Every day we have a laugh as if we couldn't care less about anything. But it's all a front. Deep down we're scared. There's nowhere I can say these things but in my diary, which nobody else will see. Every night, when I close my eyes, there's a pit of despair in my stomach, that I'm in this alone, no matter what friends I have round me. My life hangs on a thread every day. Night after night I dream of happy times without a care in the world. I have a recurring dream of home. I get off the train, walk out of the station down the road to my house. I walk in the door and feel that danger is over. Then I wake up and I know it's not, that another day has come when the enemy wants to kill me and I want to kill him. Before I get up I want to cry with frustration. Do the blokes I fly with feel the same? If they do they won't tell me. But I bet they do.

## 15 AUGUST 1940

The Jerries have changed tactics. We don't fly over the Channel every day now. Day after day, chasing bombers through clouds, duelling with Messerschmitts and seeing British ships sinking beneath us, was terrible. The weather's better now, and the Germans are bombing airfields instead, so the battles are over land. Today has been the biggest. Over and over the bombers came and the Messerschmitts with them. Sortie after sortie we flew till our fuel was low, back down to refuel, then up again. Dogfight after dogfight: narrow escapes, bullets expended into empty air, not a chance of a kill for me unless we met bombers with no fighter escort. Then it was easy. I hate what the German bombers are here to do, but I feel sorry for the poor devils having to fly those lumbering Dorniers and Heinkels which, without fighter escorts, are sitting ducks. Sergeant Dorosz, though, is having the time of his life. The squadron lost three planes, including one hit on the ground by bombs, but we downed fifteen bombers and felt the day had been a good one. Perhaps the Germans don't have as many fighters as we thought.

I have to stop writing now. I'm so tired. We can be ordered in the air at any moment, from three in the morning onwards. Tonight, we're sleeping under our Hurricanes, with parachute packs for pillows. What else can we do? We've no time to sleep in our beds any more.

# 21 AUGUST 1940

Oh, God. This has been a terrible day. We were in the air at 3.30 this morning. We were homed in on by a group of Messerschmitts escorting Junkers 88s coming in towards London. We made for the bombers and the battle started. The Messerschmitts bounced us from above and then it was all a blur. I don't know if I got a fighter, as I turned out of his way and hit him with a burst of machine gun fire, but I do know that I never saw him again. But a sudden jolt told me that I was hit. The smoke cleared. I saw David's plane in front. Suddenly a Messerschmitt was on his tail. I don't think David saw him. I screamed, "Watch out!" but what use was that? The next thing I knew, there was a sudden orange flare from his wing right by the cockpit. He went out of control and the wing just broke off. I saw David's Hurricane twisting helplessly to the ground, until it exploded below me. He had no time to parachute out. I could only hope he was dead before he went through those last few seconds. I chased the Messerschmitt that got him, but he was too fast for me. I was hit myself and had to land.

I've lost friends before, like Dai, but David was different. I taxied to a halt, scrambled out and found tears streaming down my face. The ground crew rushed up. My plane is unserviceable: there aren't any in reserve.

I feel I don't want to fly tomorrow, except to avenge David.

What about Shirley? Someone's got to tell her.

# 22 AUGUST 1940

Last night I went to The Dog and Partridge. There's a little snug off the public bar, where David and Shirley met each night. I looked inside. Shirley was sitting on her own, waiting.

I took a deep breath, went in and sat beside her.

I didn't have to speak. "David's dead, isn't he?" she said.

"Who told you?" I answered. What a silly thing to say.

"I just knew," she answered. "I've been expecting it every day since I met him."

I didn't know what to say. "Tell me what happened," she said. I drew breath to speak, already deciding how I would tone down the truth, but then she said, "Tell it truthfully. Don't miss anything out."

So I did, and she listened. The only thing I said that might not have been true was:

"He was dead at once. He didn't know anything before he hit the ground."

"I'm glad," she said.

I got her a drink and we sat together for hours, hardly saying a word. At closing time I offered to walk her home. She answered, "Thank you, but I'd rather be alone now."

Before I left, she grasped my hand. "Johnny, don't you be next," she said.

I haven't felt so low for years. I'd rather risk my life every day than bring that news to somebody David loved and I think such a lot of.

## 23 AUGUST 1940

No flying for the squadron today. We lost five planes and three pilots yesterday, including Sergeant Dorosz. Three more planes need repairs. We have to wait for replacements. Besides, we need a rest.

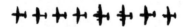

## 24 AUGUST 1940

Today has been more dreadful that any day in the air. At midday, the air-raid warnings sounded. Soon we heard the inevitable roar and saw about forty Junkers 88s approaching. The anti-aircraft guns opened up and suddenly a squadron of Spitfires from airfields north of

London was overhead. We didn't run for the air-raid shelters: I don't know why. We just stood, looked up and watched fascinated, as someone else did the work for us. We saw about ten Junkers downed, but still the rest flew on until they were overhead. Then the bombs rained down, and still we stood there. I heard a shout: "Get under cover, you fools!" Everybody jumped into life and ran for the shelters. But I couldn't move. I just watched.

I saw four Hurricanes hit, and direct hits on the control tower, the sergeants' Mess and then, oh my God, the main air-raid shelter. Then, the bombers were gone. I watched the Spits chase them, getting another couple as they went.

It was suddenly very quiet. I'd stayed in the open, because right then I couldn't care less what happened to me, yet I'd escaped without a scratch. I didn't even feel the blast, though all around was destruction. I wondered how many had died in that air-raid shelter and how many of us flyers survived. It was safer in the air after all.

Was I destined to lead a charmed life in this Air Force after all? Never. No chance.

The noise of fire engines and ambulances was broken by a new engine noise. I knew it well enough – a Junkers. One was coming in at about fifty feet. It looked as if it was doing a low level bombing run. I threw myself on the ground – and then heard this colossal shriek of metal and a rending crash not thirty yards away. I scrambled up again. The Junkers had crashed, nose up. Low level bombing my foot.

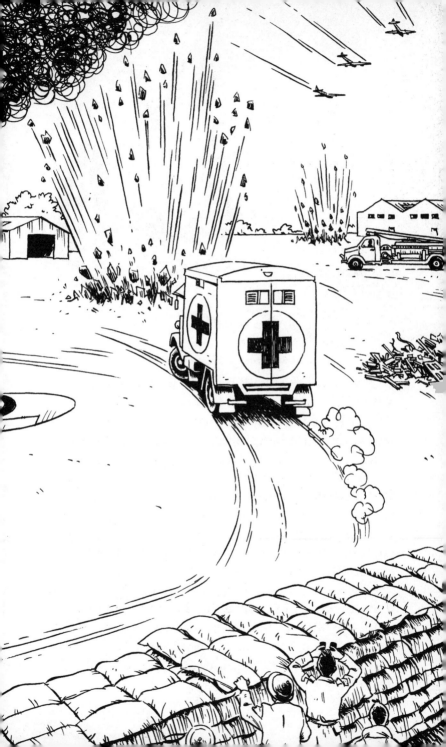

Someone must still be alive in it. He might be
a pilot like me. I rushed to the cockpit. I forgot
that any second this thing could blow up. I
found the pilot hanging upside down in his seat,
held in by his straps. I eased the straps off. He
was alive, but wounded. I dragged him out and
laid him on the grass. And then I looked up, to
see a machine-gun pointing straight at me from a
turret and a gunner watching me, ready to fire. I
shouted, "Don't shoot, I'm helping your friend!"
But still he aimed at me.

The smell of petrol, oil and something else was
overpowering. I saw dead bodies in the plane.
Only the pilot and gunner had survived – and the
gunner, like a good Nazi, was fighting to the end.

I came back to the pilot and tried to staunch

the blood of his wound. Surely the gunner wouldn't shoot when I was helping his friend? Then I was aware that an ambulance had driven up and the medics were with me.

"All right, mate," one said. "We'll take over."

"Watch out for that machine-gunner," I said.

"What for?" said another medic. "He'll never fire another shot. He's dead."

I didn't feel relieved. I felt sick.

# 25 AUGUST 1940

The squadron's finished. The airfield's out of action. Somehow the Post Office Engineers kept the telephones working so we continued for a while, though we lost five more planes on the ground. The other Biggin Hill Hurricane squadron had nowhere to land because of bomb craters all over the runways, so they were diverted somewhere else and there they'll stay. But what happened to the people has been terrible. Everyone – officers, airmen, civilian staff – who'd gone to the main air-raid shelter, was killed. Most in the other shelters survived, but that's still half the airfield's personnel dead. Three pilots were killed.

We're way below strength, and we've no planes left so we'll be stood down until the squadron can be re-formed. Which means, thankfully, a few days leave.

# 29 AUGUST 1940

Home last night, after a slow, crowded train journey. Dad met me. He'd got a few gallons of petrol, though he wouldn't say how because it's rationed. I'm surprised he hasn't laid the car up for the duration of the war. The headlights were taped over with little slits showing. We drove down dark streets at five miles an hour. Twice Air Raid Wardens stopped us, but when Dad wound his window down they said, "Oh, it's you, Mr Hedley. Sorry," and Dad answered, "No, you're quite right. You can't be too careful."

Mum was so pleased to see me and so was my sister Janet, who says she'll join the Wrens – the Women's Royal Naval Service – when she's old enough, which made Dad start singing *A Life on the Ocean Wave*.

Being home was wonderful – so peaceful. But then we heard the wail of the air-raid sirens and that sinister, throbbing drone in the air: the bombers were coming. I felt so helpless. I should be in the air protecting my family, but all I can do is crouch in the Anderson shelter with them, and hope the bombs don't land on us.

# 1 SEPTEMBER 1940

Back on duty again. Of our sector airfields, only Tangmere and Kenley are still serviceable. I'm to be posted to a Spitfire squadron north of London, at RAF North Weald, in Essex. I go tomorrow.

I wanted to tell Shirley, but I hadn't got a

phone number. So this evening I went to The Dog and Partridge for a farewell drink with such mates as were left. I looked into the snug, and I saw her, sitting in the same place.

I joined her. She looked up and smiled. "I heard you were on leave," she said. "I knew you'd be back soon."

I told her I'd been posted to North Weald. "I'm leaving too," she answered. "I'm joining the Waafs – the Women's Auxiliary Air Force. Perhaps we'll meet up somewhere."

Then I knew I really hoped we would. If she's joining the Waafs, this chaotic war will probably throw us together again somewhere.

She must have read my thoughts. "I hope so too," she said.

## 2 September 1940

So I have to get used to a new fighter and new colleagues. Strange – all this time and I've never flown a Spitfire. The Hurricane is sleek and streamlined and I love it because it served me well, but I must admit the Spitfire is something else completely. Those strange-shaped, nearly pointed wings, that bubble of a cockpit, a body so smoothly in proportion that you know its design is perfect. I flew one for the first time today. This must be what a jockey feels riding a Derby winner. I could throw it around the sky so easily, accelerate so much faster than the old Hurricane, climb more steeply, feel the power in her. When I landed, I got out and said aloud, "Right, you Jerries. Here I come."

I've come with a promotion. I'm Flying Officer now. So who's in the squadron with me? Well, we've got a South African squadron leader, a Frenchman, three Australians, two Poles and the rest are English.

And guess who else is here? Jim Bassett. Yes, my friend and David's friend, now a sergeant-pilot with a medal for bravery. We were overjoyed to meet each other. But – this is the RAF. I'm an officer and he's only a sergeant, so we can't go for a drink together, can't be friends, except when we're flying and depending on each other to stay alive.

But I did manage to tell him about David. He was quiet for a moment, then said, "He was a good bloke. I liked him." Who could say more?

## 23 SEPTEMBER 1940

I think my war may be over. I'm in a hospital near Cambridge, with a left leg in a mess and a Spitfire in pieces in a field. Even the Civilian Repair Organisation won't find enough bits fit to use to patch up another plane. Eight days ago, September 15th, was my worst so far. I should be dead. It's only thanks to – no. I've got to tell the story from the start.

✈ ✈ ✈ ✈ ✈ ✈ ✈ ✈

We took off early that morning. Huge masses of enemy aircraft were approaching London. Now we were part of the "big wing", new tactics dreamed up by Douglas Bader, a pilot with no legs who'd been shooting down Germans all summer. This meant that the squadrons formed up together. I reckoned if I were the enemy and saw all us lot coming towards him, two hundred planes at a time, it would scare me stiff. But this is the Luftwaffe we're fighting, and nothing seems to scare them. Still, we'll give it a try.

We've got new orders. Hurricanes are to attack bombers, Spitfires attack fighters. Strewth! There must have been four times as many German fighters as bombers. The Luftwaffe wasn't taking any chances. Once we were among them, it was every man for himself.

Some of us believe in attacking head-on. Not me. I haven't got the nerve. If either misjudge the time to pull away, you can collide head on at a combined speed of nearly 800 miles an hour. At least you wouldn't know much about it. Jim has the knack of pulling away at the precise split-second and raking the Messerschmitt with bullets from above or below, usually making a kill. He's met no German pilot as good at it. Yet.

45

The first Messerschmitt I saw go down went like that. I saw Jim break away from our formation, go straight for a Messerschmitt, climb over it just when the enemy pilot must have lost his nerve and fire on it from above. It spun to the ground, black smoke pouring out of it. I saw a parachute floating to the ground and felt glad. At least in a Spitfire I won't be surprised from above. I can dive on Messerschmitts now. So I climbed, saw five Messerschmitts below me and dived on them, firing as I went. I know I hit one, though it didn't seem in any trouble – not yet, anyway. I nearly got another, but the pilot did a tight turn and then was chasing me. I saw his cannon shell streak past my wing. So I made a tight turn myself, ended up underneath him and tried another burst. I saw bullet holes in his fuselage and smoke pouring out. He was a goner for sure. I'll claim two kills when I get back, I thought. Then it changed to "if I get back" because suddenly the plane rocked and buffeted. Cannon shells had hit me. I felt a searing pain in my right leg; I saw blood seeping away. Three Messerschmitts were on me. I was easy meat.

My leg was numbing fast. I tried to dive out of the Jerries' way but they wouldn't let me go. I was losing blood and getting weaker. I hadn't even the strength to push the cockpit cover open and parachute out.

But then, diving right across and making a tight turn towards the Messerschmitts came a Spitfire. I saw the letters on the fuselage – it was Jim's. I heard machine-gun fire, saw a

Messerschmitt hurtling to the ground trailing smoke and then the other two making off as fast as they could. They were off back to France while they still had some fuel.

Then Jim was by my side, waggling his wings and motioning me through his cockpit window to follow him.

I don't know how I managed to land. I could hardly stay conscious: I had to follow Jim. As we approached North Weald his Spitfire was a dim shadow-plane and I don't remember anything else. All I know is that I pranged the Spitfire in a field and was unconscious when an Air Raid Warden pulled me out. All I know, that is, except for one thing. Jim had guided me home and saved my life.

I was unconscious for two days. I've smashed up my leg – they took a whole cannon shell out of it and I might have to lose it. I was filled up with pints of new blood. I reckon there's none left that I was born with.

I'm so tired. I have to sleep.

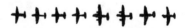

## 23 SEPTEMBER 1940

My parents were allowed to visit me. They didn't stay long – they had a difficult journey back. They didn't know whether to be sad about my leg or thankful I was alive. "Blow the leg," I said. "I can live without it."

# 1 OCTOBER 1940

Jim came. He breezed into the ward in civilian clothes saying, "Now then, Johnny, none of this officer nonsense, neither of us are in uniform." I was thankful. "Good old Jim," I said.

Then I remembered I had a lot more to be thankful to him for. "You saved my life," I said.

"Huh!" he replied. "You'd save mine if you had to."

"I would," I said. "If it comes to it, I will." Then I asked, "Why aren't you flying?"

"It's over. I reckon we've won. Jerry hasn't been near us since. I know the weather's been foul, but that's not all. They say the boffins intercepted a message from Hitler ordering the invasion forces to pull out. Hitler's not going to invade us after all."

I just stared at him. I couldn't believe it. He slapped me on the back so hard that two nurses ran up to see if I was all right. "We've done it, mate, we've seen off Jerry!" he shouted.

I leant back on my pillow. I'd never felt so relieved or contented.

"You get that leg right and start flying again," said Jim. "Then you'll have your chance to save me like you said."

# 14 OCTOBER 1940

I didn't think I'd have any visitors today, but I did, one I'd been thinking about a lot. Shirley. I knew I shouldn't think about her.

She'd been David's girl.

I don't want to seem a scavenger.

She was in Waaf's uniform – like all new recruits, Aircraftswoman 2nd class, the RAF's lowest of the low. She walked up the ward to me and kissed me on the forehead. "Oh, Johnny, thank God you didn't die as well," she said.

I didn't know what to say. For a while I looked at her stupidly.

Her face fell. "Don't you want to see me?" she asked.

"Of course I do. It's just that…"

"I know," she said. "Don't think about it."

More silence. Then she said, "I'm working in the admin block at West Raynham in Norfolk. I'm only a clerk. I may as well have stayed at home. But I've applied to become an officer. I'm being posted away."

"Our ways might cross again," I said.

There was a rather strained silence. I had to

speak, or she might go. "You heard Jim Bassett saved my life?" I said, and then could have bitten my tongue out. If he could save mine, why couldn't I save David's?

"I heard," she said. "He's a brave man." Then: "I wish we women could do something more than sit in an office all day."

We didn't say much afterwards and I almost felt relieved when the sister said, "Time's up, I'm afraid."

But now the time was here I didn't want Shirley to go. As she left, I wondered if I'd ever see her again. Now I know I really want to.


# 15 DECEMBER 1940

So long since I last wrote in this diary. But so much has happened. Thank God, I didn't need to have the leg off, so I won't be another Douglas Bader. I can walk, just about, and I'll always have a limp. I've been convalescing and getting stronger, though I'll never play football again.

But I may fly again soon. Not fit for operational duties at first, but I can wait. I'd like to be posted to an OTU, an Operational Training Unit, as an Instructor. Chaps who've learnt to fly will get the feel of Spits and Hurricanes, Beaufighters and Blenheims, be trained in basic battle techniques and then go out to fill up the squadrons. Fighter Command will have a different job now. If Hitler won't invade us, perhaps we've got him on the run. We'll go and find him. We'll take the fight to the enemy.

## 4 APRIL 1941

When Jim said the Luftwaffe hadn't been near
us, he was too optimistic. No sooner was the
Battle of Britain over than the Blitz – heavy
night bombing aimed at people, not airfields or
factories – really started. I know all about it, not
only by what I hear on the wireless and read in
the papers, but by what I'm told. I see again
how much better it is to be fighting, doing
something positive, than lying in a shelter
wondering if the next bomb is for you.
Thankfully, no bombs have come near where
I'm convalescing in the Cotswolds, but I often
feared for my parents – and for Shirley. But Jim
tells me – and it's strictly hush-hush – that these
powerful new Beaufighters have their own
radar sets so they find the German bombers for
themselves. At last they can see them off.

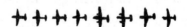

# 10 APRIL 1941

I'm cleared off convalescence, passed fit to fly, and the posting to an Operational Training Unit in the Cotwolds as an instructor has come through. And I'm promoted to Flight-Lieutenant. I'm living again.

# 20 JULY 1941

It's wonderful to be at the controls of a Hurricane again. Now it's the turn of the young lads I'm instructing. It's hardly two years since I first flew the dear old Tiger Moth, yet I feel an old man in comparison. The new boys have mainly come from the RAF Flying Schools in Canada, where most recruits are sent for training now. I think seeing England again is a shock to them. They've not come back at a good time. The war isn't going well. I hear reports of a new, deadly German fighter, the Focke-Wulf 190, better than anything we've got. Now we're finding what the Germans found last year, that fighting over enemy territory isn't funny. Escorting bombers to their targets isn't a piece of cake either. Deep down, I can't help feeling relieved I'm out of it for a while. But I'll keep that to myself.

Besides, the new kids look at me with some awe. They know I fought through the Battle of Britain, so I'm one of Mr Churchill's "few", who stood alone to keep the Jerries out when nobody else was left.

# 15 SEPTEMBER 1941

I can't believe it. Shirley's arrived at the unit!
She's got through her training: she's a Flight-
Officer working in administration.

"Did you wangle this somehow?" I asked her.

"Pure chance," she answered. "Strange things
happen in the RAF."

You can say that again. But sometimes things
can be nice ones. Here was a chance. I might not
get another. "There's a dance in the Officer's
Mess next week. Will you be my partner?"

She gave a radiant smile which made my
heart race. "Of course I will, Johnny," she replied.

# 14 OCTOBER 1941

I've bought a little car. It's an old black Ford, but
it chugs along nicely. When our off-duty periods
coincide, I take Shirley for long drives round the
Cotswolds, through places with lovely English
names: Shipton-under-Wychwood, Bourton-on-
the-Water. Sometimes we stop the car and walk,
letting the keen fresh air clear our minds of
terror and danger.

Today, when I stopped the car between
Witney and Burford and we got out, she spoke
frankly about David. "I loved him," she said.
"If he'd got through the war I'd have married
him. I'll never forget him. But he's gone now and
he can't come back. We have to live ourselves,
Johnny."

"If we stay alive, life will be all the sweeter,"

I replied. "We'll really value what we've got."

"I know," she said and linked arms in mine as we walked back to the car. I've thought much about that conversation since, and I have a feeling that a lot was meant under the simple words we said.

## 23 DECEMBER 1941

Christmas is here again. I'm off home for some leave tonight. But for two pins I'd have stayed, because Shirley's being kept back on duty. Yes, things have gone well between us. But I must see my parents and Janet. There'll be plenty of time to introduce them to Shirley.

# 19 APRIL 1942

At last. I'm passed fit for operational duties again.
I've lived a soft life on training duties, where the
only danger is pranging a kite through bad luck
or incompetence, and going out with Shirley.

We have an understanding now. Several
times I've wondered whether to ask her to
marry me. But it's not fair. If she says "Yes" it
may be because she's sorry for me going back
into the fray. I might be killed. If she says "No"
and I am killed, she'd feel bad for the rest of her
life because if she hadn't, at least I'd have died
happy. I won't give her such a decision.

# 7 JUNE 1942

The posting's through. I'm going to Duxford,
near Cambridge, to a squadron equipped with a
new plane I've heard a lot about. The Hawker
Typhoon, the "Tiffie". It can go faster than the
dreaded Focke-Wulf 190. It has cannon instead
of machine guns – much more powerful. It's the
answer to our prayers.

# 15 June 1942

I've just had my first sight of a Typhoon. I was
amazed. It's a single-engined, single-seater like
the Spit and the old Hurricane – but it's huge.

Tonight in the Mess hasn't cheered me up
much. The other pilots seemed determined to
put the fear of God in me. Apparently the
Typhoon is a pig to fly. The cockpit doors are
liable to fly off. Because of its thick wings, built
so it can hold four cannon and still stay stable, it
can't manoeuvre well over 15,000 feet. Not much
use against the Focke-Wulf 190. Worst of all, the
tail falls off. Nobody knows why, not even the
boffins. Two identical planes can go into steep
dives together, getting up to top speed. One pulls
out with no trouble, the tail of the other drops off
and it flies straight into the ground.

Still, an Australian pilot said to me, "Don't
worry, cobber. The Tiffie may scare you, but it
scares the Germans more." I don't know if that
makes me feel much happier.

# 12 July 1942

I'm getting the knack of the Tiffie. It's a powerful
brute. Its speed and acceleration smash you back
in your seat. It's no good as a fighter, but it can
fly very fast at low altitudes. Nothing can come
near it. And the Spitfire's been improved.
They've made it into a new plane to match the
Focke-Wulf, by giving it a bigger engine and a
4-bladed propeller. Sometimes I wish I was

flying it myself.

We fly low-level patrols over the North Sea and the Channel looking out for German "Jabos", tip-and-run fighters with a couple of bombs slung under the wings, flying so low that radar can't pick them up. It's alarming to see your propellor leaving a wake in the sea at 400 miles an hour because you're so low.

It's also a drawback that some idiot gunners in the Army and Navy think we're Germans. So, I'm ashamed to say, do some of our Spitfire squadrons. A few Tiffies have been shot down by our own people. They mistake us for Focke-Wulf 190s. Are they blind?

We're getting black and white stripes on our wings so nobody can mistake us again.

# 6 AUGUST 1942

Rumours of something big afoot. We're practising strafing targets on the ground and low level bombing with bombs slung under the wings. What's it all for?

# 18 AUGUST 1942

We've just had a briefing. I'm writing these thoughts down before I snatch a few hours' sleep. Our target is a French Channel port, Dieppe. It's a big operation, with Navy, Army and Air Force going in together. We dive-bomb it, the Navy shells it, Army Commandos go in and capture it. The biggest thing since the Battle of Britain. Does it mean we'll be going back to France soon and driving the Germans out?

# 19 AUGUST 1942

We took off at dawn. The whole force joined up over the Channel. Above us were more Spitfires than I ever thought to see in the air at one time. Lower were the Hurricanes and Whirlwinds.

Below us were landing craft and ships. "Watch out, Jerry," I thought. "We're on the way back."

But soon it was mayhem all around and below. The Luftwaffe were determined to break our air shield. Focke-Wulfs and Messerschmitts were diving in. The flak was deadly: I'd never seen so much anti-aircraft fire. We were soon split up. I came in as low as I dared and peered through the smoke for targets. I saw a German gun installation firing into the air. I did a low run and strafed them with cannon shells, turned and came back to repeat the dose. Their guns stopped firing. Now it was time to get out of here or I'd run out of fuel on the way home. I flew low across a railway marshalling yard and strafed a few locomotives, then climbed and went like a bat out of hell home.

Back at Duxford I refuelled, rearmed and took off again. Now Dieppe was just a pall of smoke.

I couldn't see what was happening beneath me.
The anti-aircraft fire – "flak" – was still bad. I
tried to come in low, looking for German guns
and ships in the harbour. But now I was afraid of
hitting our own commandos. This was awful. I
saw no other British aircraft. I was on my own. I
climbed and saw a Focke-Wulf coming straight at
me. This was Jim Bassett's favourite tactic, which
always scared me stiff. I loosed a few more
rounds of cannon shell at him, then climbed and
scooted off home again like a frightened rabbit. I
didn't wait to see if I'd got him.

I was thankful when I was back at Duxford
again. This has been a very dodgy day. Three of
us haven't come back, including my Australian.
I was getting ready for another sortie when the
order came through – stand down: the operation
is over, the troops are withdrawn, with 3,000

dead or taken prisoner by the Germans. We've lost a lot of planes – perhaps some of the lads I trained. Whatever the top brass were trying to do, it hasn't worked.

## 6 NOVEMBER 1942

Sometimes we fly without bombs, in pairs or alone, across the Channel into Northern France looking for freight trains carrying German tanks and guns. When we see one, we chase it and strafe it with cannon shells. Usually the locomotive comes off the track and the train with it. To have the lot go into a river or over an embankment is especially pleasing. It's like being a kid again, playing with my model railway. You forget real people are driving them. Perhaps the driver and fireman are French. They're not enemies. They didn't ask the Germans to occupy their country and they haven't got much choice but to drive the enemy's trains. It's a problem.

Otherwise, shooting up freight trains is good sport, and relatively safe for us as well. For some unfathomable reason, these jaunts are called "rhubarbs".

## 30 DECEMBER 1942

The end of another year. And the war seems no nearer ending.

I've had a good leave over Christmas and the New Year. Christmas at home was a haven of peace: New Year with Shirley was marvellous. We saw the New Year in together and hoped for better times.

"I'd like to ask you to marry me," I said.

"Why don't you?" she replied.

"It wouldn't be right," I said. "I don't want you to be a war widow or to make a mistake."

"Johnny," she replied. "I'm not making a mistake. If you're killed, I know I'm losing a lifetime of happiness. But at least I can say I was your wife and I would be proud."

"Are you sure about this?" I said.

"Of course I am," said Shirley.

I rummaged through my pockets, hoping I might find something which would do as a temporary engagement ring. Nothing. So I took a clean handkerchief, tied it round her finger so it looked like she'd cut herself, went down on one knee and said, "Shirley, will you marry me?"

"Of course I will," she answered.

I'll buy an engagement ring as soon as the shops open.

## 31 January 1943

We've just got married, in the church at Biggin Hill near Shirley's home. Only family there, Shirley's and mine. We wore our best uniforms and afterwards had a family meal made from everybody's saved-up rations and a few special items which you don't often see nowadays. Nobody asked where they came from!

No honeymoon. A night together in the guest room at The Dog and Partridge, then back to our camps early in the morning. Our first years of married life will be spent separated by the RAF.

## 28 MARCH 1943

Three months of the year gone already and I've not seen Shirley since we were married. We've been doing more night "rhubarbs", still after freight trains, since the Germans seem to be sending most of their goods by night now. We also escort bombers looking for shipping to attack. Compared with those disastrous days in 1940, life flying the Typhoon is almost a rest cure.

We're helped by being so fast at low altitudes and using cloud to hide from the enemy and scare him stiff when we suddenly appear. Yes, we lose a few Tiffies. But we feel we're winning.

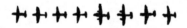

## 15 JUNE 1943

I don't know much about admin and reorganisation and most of the time I don't care, but this is important. It seems that we Typhoon squadrons are now part of what they call a Tactical Air Force. What does that mean? Not just a raid, like Dieppe. We're gearing up for a full invasion. We're going to drive the Germans out of France – one day soon. We're on the move at last. We can win this war soon.

# 20 JULY 1943

Strange. We've waited a month and there's no difference. We still go rhubarbing. We've lost six planes and four pilots in the last month – for those who don't know what they're doing, rhubarbs are pretty dangerous. Replacement pilots arrive all the time.

# 8 AUGUST 1943

I might have known it. War can do strange and wonderful things. Jim Bassett is HERE, transferred from Spitfires. My best RAF mate still alive. What's more, he's been promoted. He's a Flying Officer. About time too. A medal and a commission – he deserves them both.

# 16 AUGUST 1943

If there's anyone I want to do a rhubarb with, it's Jim. We trust each other so completely. Tonight we get our wish. The usual targets – trains and army convoys. The Germans are wise to rhubarbs now. We don't often get attacked: they haven't many planes left. But their flak is deadly.

# 10 SEPTEMBER 1943

I've not been able to bring myself to write about what happened on that last rhubarb with Jim until now.

We took off at 9.00 on a clear night with a rising moon. We came over low as usual, skimming the waves and came in over the Normandy coast east of Rouen. As always, the flak started up and we climbed fast to escape it. We looked for the main railway line to Paris. We saw a freight train loaded with tanks and big guns and set about it together. I went for the locomotive, Jim the trucks. We caused very satisfying damage. But the train wasn't undefended. Troops swarmed out of the trucks and set up machine guns and light anti-aircraft guns. When the firing at us started I signalled to Jim that it was time to go. But suddenly my Tiffie wouldn't climb. I hauled back on the stick. Nothing. I had no controls. A lucky Jerry bullet had severed something. There was only one thing to do. Bale out, though the ground was perilously close. I pushed back the cockpit cover, felt a rush of cold air, scrambled out and pulled my parachute's ripcord at once. Mercifully, it opened and brought me to the ground with a nasty bump.

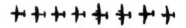

I was in a field next to a wood. Jim's Tiffie was overhead. "Go home, you fool!" I wanted to shout, but he wouldn't hear and I didn't know who else might. I had an odd thought – I'd spent half the last three years flying over enemy territory, but never stood on it before. How was I going to get out of this mess?

I heard a roaring in the sky. The moon had risen now and in its light I saw those familiar silhouettes – three Messerschmitts. I knew who they were after – Jim. I hoped he was well out of here.

I heard the chatter of gunfire. I prayed it wasn't at Jim, or that the guns were his and he'd disposed of the Messerschmitts. But then I saw all three flying low, as if they were looking for someone.

I felt cold. I couldn't believe they'd shot him down. I peered upwards for a glimpse of a parachute coming down, but didn't see one. Then I thought – they'll know I'm round here. I've got to hide.

I ran for the wood. I bundled the parachute up, hid it under a thick carpet of rotting leaves and tried to make myself difficult to find. Then I thought better of it. German soldiers would be looking. I thought I heard motor bikes and lorries coming near. I wouldn't last an hour. We'd been told what to do in these situations, but it seemed different on the ground. The roar of their bikes came nearer. Then, to my horror, two German soldiers on motor bikes crossed the field, plain to see in the moonlight. Then came a large van, followed by a Mercedes car and, to show they never missed a trick, a low-loader for my wrecked plane. The back doors of the van opened and two doghandlers jumped out, with Alsatians. The dogs' baying chilled me. Someone in civilian clothes who looked, even from here, very sinister, got out of the Mercedes.

There was only one thing to do. I struck deeper into the wood, further and further, not caring about low branches, tree roots and brambles. I don't know how long I kept going. It felt like hours. I was afraid I was going round in a circle and would come back to where I started. But then I came to the wood's end and a farm track. It was 5.00 in the morning and getting light. I was just thinking this was about the time farmers usually get up when I saw a horse and cart approaching. Should I hide again? It must be a French farmer – but he might be collaborating with the Germans. I hid again to watch the cart pass by. But the farmer drew in the reins, got down and said, "I know you're there, *Monsieur l'aviateur Anglais*. I'm your friend."

+ + + + + + + +

I'd rather trust him than the Nazis. I came out from the trees. He said, "Jump on the cart and put this old army greatcoat on. I wore it in the last war." I put it on and sat beside him. He spoke enough English and I had enough French for us to communicate. "I'm in the Resistance, the Maquis," he said. "We'll get you back to England." What wonderful words. For the first time I dared to think about Shirley.

We jogged along as the sun rose. "Your name now is Alphonse. You are my son," he said. "Alphonse was a soldier when the Germans invaded. He was killed. I have his working clothes still."

Hearing this, I couldn't speak. The farmer continued: "I'm glad you say nothing. From now on you must pretend you're deaf and dumb."

We reached the farmhouse. The farmer's wife fed me with coffee and new bread, the farmer produced the clothes and I put them on. Then he took away my uniform. "I'll burn this and bury the brass badges," he said. Soon my uniform and flying jacket was a pile of ash.

"But if the Germans find me, I'll be shot," I said.

"They won't find you," he answered. "You'll have papers which the Germans won't suspect. You just keep quiet. But they will try to make you speak. Be on your guard." Then he said, "Another British plane was shot down last night."

"My friend," I answered.

"That's war," he said. "Now you and I will load the cart with turnips to take to town. Once there, I'll hand you over to someone else who'll get you to the coast."

"Do I hide under the turnips?" I asked when the cart was loaded.

"No hiding," he replied. "You're Alphonse."

"Someone is coming," said the farmer's wife.

The same motorbikes, van and car that I saw the night before roared into the farmyard. Six soldiers and the two Alsatians came out of the van. Someone else was with the soldiers, his arms tied behind his back. Jim. The sinister, black-coated civilian I had seen before climbed out of the Mercedes, followed by a tall Luftwaffe officer.

"We're looking for a British airman," the civilian said. "If you know where he is, you'd better say."

"He is not here," said the farmer.

The civilian came up and stood very close to me. "Who is this, then?" he said

"My son," said the farmer.

"Can't he speak for himself?" shouted the civilian.

"Deaf and dumb since birth."

The civilian motioned a soldier up to him and nodded. The soldier lifted his boot and brought it down as hard as he could on my foot. I bit my tongue and let out nothing but a grunt of pain. Then he bent close to my ear and screamed at the top of his voice. I didn't flinch.

How I managed those things I'll never know, except that this was what the farmer must mean by trying to make me speak. If I'd let loose a few English swear-words, I'd have a bullet in my head at once. The civilian stared hard at me, then said, "Very well." For God's sake don't look at me, Jim, I thought. Thankfully he made no sign of noticing me. But the civilian said, "You see, we've found one Englishman already."

He took a revolver from his overcoat pocket and held it to the back of Jim's neck. "And now he pays the price of all enemies of the Third Reich." His fingers tightened on the trigger.

It was all I could do not to shout, "You murderer! He's in uniform." But I had to stay dumb.

Strange, someone was saying it for me, in

71

perfect English. The tall Luftwaffe officer. "You
have no right. This is against the rules of war.
Surely even the Gestapo are still civilised?"

The civilian put his revolver back in his
pocket. "Very well, Herr Colonel," he said. "I
will do as you say. But he is my prisoner now."

"See that he stays so. I'm watching you."

They left. We heard cars and motorcycles roar
off.

My heart was thumping. "What if they'd
asked for papers?" I said.

"The papers are here," said the farmer. "They
were my son's. He's left this farm four times in
the last two years."

What could he mean?  His son had been killed.
Then I realised. I wasn't the first British airman
he'd helped. But Jim would have been shot if not
for that officer. I'd wanted to shout "Thank you"
to him. But I had to be deaf and dumb and
I wanted desperately to get back home.

Well, I did go home. It was a scary experience. One day, when I've got time, I'll write a book about it. The farmer took me to market, another Resistance man drove me in a little Renault van to the next town and then, moving by night and being handed from one member of the Maquis to another, I reached a little fishing village three days later, was bundled onto a fishing boat and run by night across the Channel. After establishing who I was and a long debriefing with the Intelligence people, I was back at base with a long tale to tell. I won't write in this diary again until we go back to France properly.

Meanwhile, I'm being sent home on leave. I need it.

# 1 JUNE 1944

Only now I'm back at Duxford can I write in my
diary. I've had a lot of time to make sense of what
happened to me in France. But now we all know
it's coming – D-Day, Day of Decision, will be here
in the next few days. The liberation of France.
The longed for invasion – the Second Front, to
take the strain off the Russians in their terrible
war with Germany in the east. The troops, ships
and planes are ready, British, American and their
Allies, waiting for the signal to go. Our Tiffies are
now fitted with rockets – very potent weapons.

I've seen Shirley a few times. It's been
difficult. But we know this is the most
dangerous part of the war, even more so than
the Battle of Britain. When we said goodbye last
time we both had a fear that it might be for ever.

# 5 JUNE 1944

When will D-Day come? We've waited and
waited and the weather gets worse – storms,
driving rain, low cloud, heavy seas.

# 10 JUNE 1944

Well, D-Day came on the next day, June 6th. General Eisenhower, the Commander-in-Chief, gave the word – a brave thing, because the weather was worse than ever. The whole huge fleet set sail at dawn and the Tiffies were among the first planes to take off. The destination is Normandy – with luck, the Germans will be taken by surprise: we hope they expect the invasion to be near Calais. Our jobs are first, to defend the invasion force, second, to make rocket attacks on tanks and enemy installations.

Operation Overlord started, at the crack of dawn. The sky was full of planes: fighters and bombers, British and American. Beneath us on the sea were fleets of landing craft packed with soldiers. We flew over the ships, to defend them against enemy fighter-bombers. But there were hardly any. The Germans were being taken by surprise.

# 12 JUNE 1944

Back at base after a day making rocket attacks on enemy tanks and gun positions in Normandy. The fighting on the ground has plainly been terrible. But we're doing our best to get at the German army. They're sending fighters up against us now. We've got rockets and bombs strapped under our wings, but the Tiffie's a strong plane and we disposed of three Messerschmitts and lost none of ours today.

# 17 JUNE 1944

I think we're winning, just about. But when we got back tonight after a day rocketing tanks, we heard a nasty rumour. The Germans are firing some sort of pilotless bomb, which travels faster than a fighter plane. Its motor cuts out over London, it drops and explodes, causing more damage than half a squadron of bombers did in the Blitz. We might be withdrawn from France to do something about them. Still, we'll cross that bridge if we come to it. We've still got this invasion to sort out.

# 30 JUNE 1944

Well, the order's through. Pity. There's a feeling we've nearly broken the enemy's back in France.

# 15 JULY 1944

So I'm back at RAF North Weald where I came from four years ago.  And we've lost our ageing, beaten-up squadron of Tiffies. I'm sad to say goodbye to that trusty plane. We're flying its successor, the Tempest. Same body, same engine: the difference is in the wings. They look more like a Spitfire's. This means it climbs faster and at high altitudes you can really throw it around the sky. There are some new-fangled jet fighters around. The Germans have one, the Messerschmitt 263. So have we, the Gloster Meteor. Some squadrons have it already. They can keep it. It's not as fast as my lovely new Tempest.

## 20 JULY 1944

Today, I saw my first flying bomb. Everyone calls them "doodlebugs" and so will I. It was a horrible thing: a nasty, crude little black plane with tiny, stubby square wings and a jet of flame and smoke coming out of its tail jet. The thought that it had no pilot and its jet engine would soon stop, it would fall, explode and kill hundreds of people made me angry. It shot along dead straight at over 400 miles an hour. But I kept up with it easily. I fired a few bursts of cannon at it and I missed. This wasn't like fighting a real plane. There was no satisfaction, no danger, no skill, no respect for the man in the cockpit. I hated it.

Soon I'd used my ammunition up. I came home feeling very frustrated.

## 25 JULY 1944

Today I got my first doodlebug. There had been talk in the Mess about how it might be possible to tip the brute over by putting your wing under its wing and spoiling its balance. "Bloody dangerous if you ask me," said an Australian pilot to me. He was right, but I couldn't shoot one down so I thought I'd try it myself.

I've no doubt he would, too.

On patrol this morning, I saw one underneath me and dived to chase it. Hitler said no fighters could catch the V1, as he called it. He was wrong. It was doing a mere 420 miles an hour: I caught it up at 450 and gave it a quick burst. Missed again. I tried three more, hit it with the last and watched it fall away and explode harmlessly on the South Downs.

No ammo left. If I saw another, I would have to try the wing tipping. Well, like a bus, another soon came along. I caught it up and got close in and side by side. My Aussie friend was right. A slight tremor in my hand and I'd go over with it. So, very carefully, though still at over 400 miles an hour, I got in close and just underneath. My left wingtip was nearly touching the thing's right wing. A very slight turn into it, a tiny lift on the wing and over it went, satisfyingly out of control, to land in a Kent field and make a big hole in it. Piece of cake.

Two in one day. I landed back at North Weald and felt more pleased at the end of a day than at any time in the war. Nobody was killed by those two doodlebugs.

## 9 SEPTEMBER 1944

We've sorted out the doodlebugs. I got thirty of them: some pilots destroyed nearly twice as many. The flying bombs won't come again. A government minister has made a speech telling us so. And I'm on leave, a whole blissful month. Mum, Dad and, most of all, Shirley.

## 12 OCTOBER 1944

Back to work. I've had a great leave. There's a feeling around that the war is on its last legs. But I mustn't get too cocky. Plenty of men were killed on the last day of the last war.

But something sinister is happening in London. There seem to have been rather a lot of gas explosions lately. Now we know what they are. The V2, a different sort of rocket, far faster than any plane. There's no defence against it.

# 1 NOVEMBER 1944

There's only one thing to do against these V2s.
Destroy their launching pads. The difficulty is
finding them. Most seem to come from German-
occupied Holland. We're flying patrols over the
Dutch coast, watching out for activity – the Nazis
are quite capable of putting the launch-pads in
the middle of towns, where bombing them
would kill hundreds of Dutch people as well.

# 15 NOVEMBER 1944

Our squadron didn't bomb V2 launch sites for
long. No sooner had we started than we were
moved to Europe. We're at Volkel in Allied-
occupied Belgium now. It's quite like old times,
meeting the Luftwaffe in the air to fend off raids
on our airfields. Except that there don't seem so
many of them. We see the old Messerschmitts –
and something new. The new German jet fighter
– it's a real handful. Most days I'm just glad to
get back in one piece. Suddenly, the end of the
war seems a long way off after all.

## 15 JANUARY 1945

Nothing seems to have changed since November,
except that American anti-aircraft guns keep
mistaking us for Germans.

But our armies are always advancing. Soon
we'll be out of here.

## 15 APRIL 1945

Who'd have thought it five years ago? We've
recaptured, one by one, the countries the
Germans occupied. Now we're finally based on

German soil, on an old Luftwaffe base at Hopsten. There's little opposition in the air now. Allied troops are driving on into Germany, the Russian army is near Berlin – surely I'll make it back alive now.

## 31 MAY 1945

It's all over, in Europe anyway, though the war against Japan still goes on. The Germans have surrendered, Hitler has killed himself (we think) and all the top Nazis – at least, those we can find – are under arrest. So what more is there to say? VE Day came – Victory in Europe. Shirley and I went down to London. We stood with the crowds in front of Buckingham Palace, saw the King and Queen, the two princesses and Mr Churchill come out on the balcony, and cheered until we were hoarse. Our war is really over.

I'll never live so intensely, so dangerously again. At least, I hope not. I loved the flying, hated the danger, mourned some of my best friends. I never want to see anything like it again.

This is Squadron-Leader Johnny Hedley, signing off.

Cheerio, folks!

## 4 JULY 1972
### MY LAST-EVER DIARY ENTRY
I never thought I would write another page in
my old wartime diary. But I must. Shirley and I
have just come home from the USA. I'd been
asked, as a Battle of Britain veteran, to take part
in a discussion of German and British fighter
tactics to an audience of US officer-cadets. So it
was also a reunion of former RAF and
Luftwaffe pilots. We met in peace as friends
who had shared the same terrible dangers. After
flying airliners for twenty years I can't believe
what I did then. But something happened at
that meeting which brought it all back. What it
said about the human race did my heart good.

✦ ✦ ✦ ✦ ✦ ✦ ✦ ✦

Before the discussion, I was chatting with a
drink to some old friends when a tall man with
iron grey hair came up to me, and said, in
faultless English, "Excuse me, but even after

forty years, I know your face so well. It's older and you're going bald, but to me you will always be the same."

I looked at him. Yes, there was something familiar there. "I know I've seen you before," I replied. "But I can't think where."

A great smile spread over his face. "There, I knew you'd heard what I said that day and I was afraid you'd answer me. Deaf and dumb my foot."

I stared at him. "I know who you are now," I cried. "You're…"

"Herr Colonel Hermann Middlestorb. And your father, I think, is not a farmer from Normandy." He laughed, then grew serious. "But your friend, whom I saved from being shot by that blasted Gestapo man, I fear he is not with us. He was taken away. That was bad for him."

I laughed. "Jim Bassett? Oh, he's here." I called him over. "Here's someone you should meet, Jim. If it wasn't for him, you'd have had a bullet in your head in that French farmyard."

Jim looked at him, speechless, then reached out and clasped his hands.

"I feared for you when that Gestapo idiot took you away," said Hermann. "You were out of my control then."

"Don't worry, I survived. Two years as a prisoner-of-war, " said Jim.

"And as for you," said Hermann, turning to me, "if that Gestapo fool had any sense he'd have seen right through you. I knew straightaway that you were no farmer's son. But I wished you luck. I was an escaped prisoner once too. It takes one to know one, as you English say. And all three of us have been fliers in combat."

He was right. Jim and I looked at each other and smiled. War's a strange thing. It had thrown up a former deadly enemy as our good friend – for life.

# FACTFILE

## THE START OF FIGHTER COMMAND

During World War I, British fighting aircraft were part of the Army, (the Royal Flying Corps) and the Navy (the Royal Naval Air Service). Not until the end of the war was the Royal Air Force established. Even then, the Navy kept the Fleet Air Arm. When the war ended, the RAF was allowed to dwindle: in 1923 there were only forty aircraft in Britain. The rest were overseas. Then the Government realised that France had 600, so the RAF started expanding, with biplanes like those of World War I.

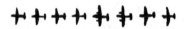

By 1936, Hitler's Germany was building an air force to dwarf all others, and war seemed likely. So the RAF was organised into Commands: Bomber Command, Coastal Command and Fighter Command. Before the war, bomber aircraft were expected to be capable of winning wars on their own. So bombers were built and fighters were ignored – except by the new chief of Fighter Command, Air Marshal Dowding. He believed that only fighters could defend Britain.

In 1938, British Prime Minister Neville
Chamberlain came back from Munich with
a treaty signed by Hitler and announced
that he had achieved, "Peace for our time."
Few people believed it; the equipment of
Fighter Command with biplanes like the
Hawker Fury and Gloster Gladiator and
then the new Spitfires and Hurricanes
started in earnest. On 3 September 1939,
war was declared. There still weren't
enough planes or pilots to match the
Luftwaffe, but without the year since
Munich, there would have been none at all.

## THE AIRCRAFT - RAF

Most people believed that biplanes, hardly
changed from the Sopwith Snipes of World
War I, were the best planes available. By
1936, German Stukas and Messerschmitt 109s
fighting for the Nationalists in the Spanish
Civil War showed that this wasn't true. Even
so, in 1936 the Gloster Gladiator, about the
most advanced biplane fighter possible, came
into service with the RAF. Dowding,
however, saw that the German Me 109s
would blow them all out of the sky.

Fortunately there were two visionary
aircraft designers working in Britain,
Sydney Camm and Reginald Mitchell.
Ignoring all the Air Ministry's "official"
requirements, both men designed their
ideal fighters. Camm worked for Hawkers
and designed the Hawker Hurricane. To

save time and money, he used a lot of parts from the old Fury biplane. But what he designed looked nothing like it. The Hurricane was a sleek, fast, single-seat, manoeuvrable plane with a retractable undercarriage and four machine guns mounted in wings strong enough to take the forces that firing them generated.

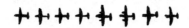

Mitchell worked for Vickers-Supermarine. He had designed the seaplane which in 1931 won the Schneider Trophy for the race to find the world's fastest seaplane. From this design the Spitfire was developed. The Spitfire was a revolutionary aircraft introducing a new age of aviation, unlike the Hurricane which was a development of the old. The shape of the Spitfire's fuselage was a model of sleekness: its curved wings made it instantly recognisable. It was built entirely of stressed metal which gave immense strength; the near-perfect design kept the Spitfire going throughout World War II. As soon as the Rolls-Royce engine it was designed around was ready, the prototype flew. The result was so extraordinary that the Air Ministry ordered it at once. But Mitchell was a sick man. He died in 1937 and never knew how his creation had helped to save his country in 1940.

So now the RAF had two fighters which could match the Messerschmitt. You can still see a Hurricane and a Spitfire flying in the Battle of Britain Memorial Flight, which often comes, together with a Lancaster heavy bomber, to air shows all over Britain.

✈ ✈ ✈ ✈ ✈ ✈ ✈ ✈

The Bolton-Paul Defiant also flew in the Battle of Britain. It looked very handsome, but had only a gun-turret behind the pilot with a gunner to fire the gun. Two-seaters were fine in World War I, but by 1940 the Luftwaffe could pick Defiants off as they saw them.

Other planes flew with Fighter Command. The Bristol Beaufighter had two engines. It was the first specialist night-fighter and with it the Luftwaffe's night raids on Britain (the "Blitz") at last had serious opposition. The Westland Whirlwind fighter-bomber had an odd-looking double fuselage. Later in the war the de Havilland Mosquito, the "wooden wonder" – which employed every carpenter de Havilland could find to build it – was a remarkable twin-engined fighter-bomber. It flew with Bomber Command as well and was the pathfinder equipped with the "Oboe" system of electronic flight guidance which helped Lancaster and Halifax bombers find their targets.

The Mosquito vied with the Spitfire, Messerschmitt 109 and Mustang for the honour of most remarkable fighter aircraft of the war. The North American Mustang was the first truly long-range fighter which at last could provide proper fighter escort deep into enemy territory.

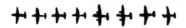

Later in the war came the Hawker Typhoon and Tempest. The Typhoon was larger than the Spitfire and Hurricane. It was meant to counter the new German Focke-Wulf 190, but it wasn't nimble enough at altitude and instead was used as a low-level attack plane, at which it was unrivalled. A bigger engine in the Spitfire proved the true rival to the Focke-Wulf. The Typhoon's development, the Tempest, had different wings which gave it the nimbleness the Typhoon lacked and remarkable speed for a piston-engined plane. These were the planes which Fighter Command and its successors flew. In 1944, the Gloster Meteor, the first British jet fighter, came into service and soon the age of the piston-engined fighting plane was over.

## THE LUFTWAFFE

Throughout 1936 the new Luftwaffe had been rehearsing for the big war to come. Picasso's famous painting *Guernica* shows the horror that bombers could cause: the shock went through the whole world. Stuka dive-bombers, with blaring sirens mounted in the wings to cause maximum terror, had struck fear everywhere.

The great designer Professor Willi Messerschmitt had designed a magnificent single-seat fighter, the Messerschmitt 109. You can see one hanging in the main hall at the Imperial War Museum in London. Messerschmitt pilots had learnt fighter tactics for monoplanes long before anybody else had. The Germans also built a huge bomber fleet, all twin-engined, of Junkers 88s, Dorniers and Heinkels.

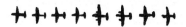

All these planes were part of a huge air force – the Luftwaffe – with Hitler's friend Marshal Hermann Goering at its head. Goering had been an air ace in World War I and now a top Nazi. Luckily for the British, his judgment was far from perfect. After France was defeated and only Britain fought on, Goering assured Hitler that he could destroy Fighter Command and leave Britain defenceless. An invasion would be easy. Hitler believed him.

## RADIO DIRECTION FINDING (RDF)
It is often thought that the British had radar in the Battle of Britain and Germany hadn't. It's not true. Germany was far

more advanced: their huge Freya and Wurzburg radar stations were better than anything the British had. Amazingly the Germans never guessed what the RDF stations along the British coast actually were.

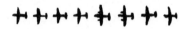

The British system was the brainchild of Robert Watson-Watt, a scientist. His slogan was "second-best tomorrow". Watson-Watt built quickly, with components already in production for radio and newly-developed television sets, a radar defence which would not be the world's greatest but which would do the job. His system could be easily repaired and, if damaged, put back into service with no delay. It worked almost perfectly. Enemy planes would be spotted massing over the English Channel: their numbers and speeds, whether fighters or bombers, and their directions were noted. The RAF interpreted the information and passed it to Fighter Command HQ, then the fighters were "scrambled". The Germans could never work out why the RAF was waiting for them as soon as they came near the coast.

## THE BATTLE OF BRITAIN

In Britain, the Battle of Britain is often viewed as a single campaign culminating in complete victory against overwhelming odds. To German historians it is nothing of the sort. It had no ending as such except the realisation that Germany wasn't going to get the air superiority Goering had promised. Fighter Command won simply by staying in existence.

Both sides lost planes at an alarming rate: the RAF replaced theirs at once. Two hundred new fighters a month and a Civilian Repair Organisation which scoured the country for damaged planes which had crash-landed kept the RAF up to strength and better.

The Germans were less efficient: their aircraft industry never really geared up for war and Hitler had other priorities. By the time of the Battle of Britain he was thinking of invading Russia, even though they had a treaty of friendship.

✈ ✈ ✈ ✈ ✈ ✈ ✈ ✈

So the Battle of Britain was a matter of industrial efficiency as much as the bravery and skill of its aircrews. This drive towards getting aircraft in the air was led by Lord Beaverbrook – Minister for Aircraft Production – with instructions from the British Prime Minister to thwart government Air Ministry red tape.

The outcome also owed much to the tactics of Air Marshal Dowding, chief of

Fighter Command, and Air Vice-Marshal Park, in charge of 11 Group. This group bore the brunt of the German attacks over Kent and Sussex. Air Vice-Marshal Trafford Leigh Mallory, in charge of 11 Group to the north of London, disliked Dowding, disagreed with everything he did and never really co-operated. Dowding made a lot of enemies: after the battle he was dismissed and Leigh Mallory took his place at the head of Fighter Command. Nowadays, most people believe Dowding's treatment was disgraceful. But the real battle was fought in the skies.There had never been an air battle like it before and it is certain there will never be one like it again.

## AFTERWARDS

The Battle of Britain was the one time when fighters held centre stage in World War II. Afterwards, British effort in the air passed to Bomber Command. By the time of the long, costly area night-bombing campaign against Germany, Fighter Command's function was effectively finished. In June 1943, part of it became ADGB (Air Defence of Great Britain): the other was subsumed into the joint British and American 2nd Tactical Air Force (TAF) gearing up for the invasion of France and the final defeat of Germany.

The ADGB had one brief hour of repeating its Battle of Britain exploits during the V1 "Doodlebug" flying-bomb campaign, when it performed wonderful feats. But it could do nothing when the V2s came and it was left to the 2nd TAF to end the threat by destroying their launchpads and the main base at Peenemunde.

But the role of British Fighters during the invasion of Europe – D-Day – and up to the German surrender was crucial. They escorted bombers and attacked enemy forces with bombs and rockets. But by 1945 the distinction between fighter and bomber aircraft was less clear. The fighter began to take on more of the bomber's functions; this distinction is even less well-defined in the modern RAF.

## JOHNNY HEDLEY

We should respect and remember what Johnny Hedley and his colleagues did all those years ago. Theirs was a unique sort of bravery, and so was that of the German pilots who opposed them. It was a vicious and cruel battle, yet fought with a sense of chivalry and mutual respect. These heroic qualities should never be exaggerated or over-glorified but equally, the sacrifices made by Johnny and others like him must never be forgotten. Truly it was what Winston Churchill called "Their finest hour."

# OTHER TITLES IN THIS SERIES

**THE DIARY OF A YOUNG ROMAN SOLDIER**
Marcus Gallo travels to Britain with his legion to help pacify the wild Celtic tribes.

**THE DIARY OF A YOUNG TUDOR LADY-IN WAITING**
Young Rebecca Swann joins her aunt as a lady-in-waiting to Queen Elizabeth the First.

**THE DIARY OF A YOUNG NURSE IN WORLD WAR II**
Jean Harris is hired to train as a nurse in a London hospital just as World War II breaks out.

**THE DIARY OF A YOUNG WEST INDIAN IMMIGRANT**
It is 1961 and Gloria Charles travels from Dominica to Britain to start a new life.

**THE DIARY OF A 1960S TEENAGER**
Teenager Jane Leachman is offered a job working in swinging London's fashion industry.

**THE DIARY OF A YOUNG ROMAN GIRL**
It is AD74 and Secundia Fulvia Popillia is helping her family prepare for her sister's wedding.

**THE DIARY OF A YOUNG MEDIEVAL SQUIRE**
It is 1332 and young William De Combe travels with his uncle to a faraway jousting competition.

**THE DIARY OF SAMUEL PEPYS'S CLERK**
It is 1665 and young Roger Scratch travels to London to work for his kinsman Pepys.